EVERYDAY MONEY $ FOR $ EVERYDAY PEOPLE

TODD CHRISTENSEN

Everyday Money for Everyday People
by Todd Christensen

© 2014 by Debt Reduction Services

Disclaimer: This publication is intended to provide accurate and authoritative information regarding personal and household financial matters. It is sold with the understanding that the author/publisher is not engaged in rendering legal, accounting, investing, or other professional services. For such services, please seek the assistance of competent and certified professionals.

To purchase copies of Everyday Money for Everyday People in large quantities at wholesale prices, please contact Aloha Publishing at alohapublishing@gmail.com

Cover design by: Cari Campbell Design
Interior design by: Fusion Creative Works
Primary Editor: Amy Larson

Print ISBN: 978-1-61206-079-8
eBook ISBN: 978-1-61206-080-4

Library of Congress Control Number: 9781612060798

Published by Aloha Publishing

ALO∂HA
PUBLISHING

Printed in the United States of America

For My All: Wendy, Riley, Grant, Ethan, and Broderick

"ALL THINGS ARE CHEAP TO THE SAVING, DEAR TO THE WASTEFUL."

—BENJAMIN FRANKLIN IN POOR RICHARD'S ALMANAC, 1734.

TABLE OF CONTENTS

PREFACE

There are plenty of smart money people and moneysmart people writing books with great suggestions and ideas to help us improve our personal and household finances. Why yet another?

Because books written for "everyday people" are few. Some books are written for or by the rich and/or the wealthy (not the same thing, by the way) or the books look and read like college texts. They're too heavy on theory and too light on the practical.

Having worked in classrooms with well over 10,000 individuals in the past ten years, it has been my privilege to learn from my students, and share with them ideas for bolstering our financial situations. This book is the outgrowth of the nearly 1,000 presentations I've facilitated over the past decade, and the conversations that occurred in those classes.

INTRODUCTION

WE, THE FINANCIALLY INSANE

Let's admit it. We're surrounded by financial insanity. We see it. We are appalled by it. We even laugh at it. But we also live it. To some degree, we all take part in it, in spite of ourselves. We overspend. We undersave. We blow through our paycheck just in time for our next paycheck. Six out of ten of us spend at least every single dollar we earn, and for many of us, we spend even more.[1]

In our heads, we know we're supposed to save for a rainy day. Yes, water heaters, cars, appliances, and televisions will all wear out, break down, or otherwise need to be replaced eventually, so we'd expect that the sane among us would be saving for those occurrences. So not so!

We know that eating out for lunch is not only less healthy than a home cooked meal, but also more expensive. So we all obviously eat healthy and affordable meals at home all the time, right? So not so! Twenty-five percent of us eat some sort of fast food EVERY day.[2]

We also know that, given the astronomical odds of winning any significant prize, dropping a few bucks on the counter for lottery tickets is literally the financial equivalent of dropping those bills straight into a crosscut shredder. So why do we, the citizens of this great nation, annually spend $178 per every man, woman, and child to purchase such tickets?[3]

Because we're financially insane! We make financially ridiculous choices with our emotions and not with our intellect. Unfortunately, doing something, even out of intuition or instinct that we know leads to a predetermined negative outcome, and yet expecting positive results, is popularly considered by many to be the very definition of insanity. We, as a society and as a nation, are guilty as charged.

Let's consider some of our less brilliant financial moves, starting with expensive borrowing options. From pawning our possessions to getting loans against the title of our vehicle to taking out what are termed payday loans, we know these options are astronomically expensive and that we're essentially shooting ourselves in the financial foot. Unfortunately, we only choose to see our immediate needs and not the medium and long-term consequences.

Take, as an example, the nice lady we'll call Evelyn, who approached one of my previous financial educators at the end of a budgeting class we were facilitating at a local nonprofit agency. Five years earlier, Evelyn shared that she had taken out three $500 payday loans to cover a short-term cash crunch. When the $575 payment for each loan came due after just two weeks (a 15–20 percent fee is typical for these loans), she owed a total of $1,725. Not surprisingly, she didn't have that much money, so the lenders offered her the chance to "roll over" her loans for another two weeks. All she needed to do was pay the same original fee for each loan (15% x $500 x 3 loans = $225) to buy herself another two weeks. Every two weeks, they offered her the same option, and every two weeks she took it. After all, doesn't it make more sense to pay $225 every two weeks than to pay $1,725 in a lump sum? She continued to roll over her three loans every two weeks for the next five years. To figure out how much she paid, simply take $225 every two weeks, multiply it by 26 two-week periods in a year, and multiply that by five years: $225 x 26 x 5 = $29,250. And guess what? She still owed the lenders the original

$1,500. Fortunately, the state has since restricted such lenders to allowing only three rollovers of the same loan.

Now, when Evelyn took out the loans, did she think she would eventually have to pay back almost twenty times the original amount of her loan? Of course not. That would be completely insane. But taking into consideration only her short-term challenges without looking down the road at the long-term consequences leads to the same insane choices.

What further adds to the frustration of financial educators like myself is the statistic that the average person taking out their first payday loan today will have taken out eight within a twelve-month period.[4]

In cases that involve such expensive borrowing options as these, I think we all agree that it's best to be below average. Certainly plenty of books exist that address the poor personal finance behaviors we exhibit in this country, so why write yet another?

First, financial education is the key to our padded room of financial insanity. At least we then have the choice to exit and find financial freedom or remain confined in our financial insanity.

Studies clearly indicate that personal finance is not being taught sufficiently in our homes. A 2011 Visa, Inc. survey found that only 46 percent of adults reported they had learned basic money management from one or both of their parents. That leaves 54 percent of those who learned about it elsewhere, mostly (38 percent) on their own.[5]

A Capital One survey of 500 graduating high school seniors from that same year shows only 22 percent of them having talked to their parents frequently about money management.[6]

The Jump$tart Coalition, of which I'm currently a state chapter president-elect, investigated state graduation requirements around the country, and only four states required a personal finance course for high school graduation. Hoorah for Missouri, Tennessee, Utah, and Virginia!

Second, the vast majority of such books are written for the medium- to high-wage earner. Even such brilliant authors and financial experts as David Bach, in The Automatic Millionaire, can use hilariously out-of-touch examples of poor consumer choices, such as that of spending over $1,000 in one afternoon on clothing, as if that's a common occurrence in the average American household. Most of us would have a hard time finding $1,000 in our checking accounts or under the credit limits of our cards to be able to make such purchases.

I generally love Suze Orman and Dave Ramsey for what they've done to push personal finance into the collective awareness of average Americans. Suze's personal story in particular is one that so many going through financial struggles can relate to. Living out of a car, waiting tables, and giving it her best, she faced sexism and a system built to take her money rather than help her grow it. Suze, you go girl!

Dave was also able to rebuild after a business bankruptcy, though most of the individuals and couples going through my bankruptcy classes might not be able to relate to anyone who had built a multimillion-dollar portfolio and support network prior to their bankruptcy.

Unfortunately, most of these books look like textbooks or novels. I know how I feel when I see such a book, in spite of an intriguing title or topic. The books look either too complex or like they are only meant to be "read" rather than "used."

I'd like this book to be easy to read (like Joel Greenblatt's *The Little Book That Beats the Market*) and easy to navigate and use (like Ric

Edelman's *The Lies about Money*). That's why this book is organized to be a guidebook, reference book, and workbook all in one. Please don't just read it. Write in it. Use it. Abuse it. Then give it as a gift to those you care about most (or maybe order a new one for them), and let the accumulation of financial literacy continue.

The Right Book for the Right People

This book is not written to help us avoid $1,000 or $10,000 shopping sprees. This book does not contain retirement or investment advice for how to take advantage of the bull market or find the silver lining in a bear market. Nor does this author have an investment tool to sell. This book is for all of those individuals and couples who have graced my classes with their smiles, their own good humor, and their obvious efforts to make the best of difficult financial situations.

This book is for you, because I know you. We've met a thousand times over the past nine years as I have facilitated presentations around the country. You've sat in my classes, shared your stories, and asked me questions you never thought of or even felt comfortable asking.

You are every man and every woman.

You are employed full-time and, while not rich, you don't believe anyone would refer to yours as a low-income household. You know you earn an average salary, perhaps even better, but feel it's never going to be enough. No matter how hard you try, your income seems insufficient for your needs and those of your family.

You may even feel it's not fair that you work so hard for your modest income while others seem to have it all. Even working hard and taking on overtime doesn't seem to help. There's never enough money.

You've probably experienced the frustration of feeling just when you're getting control of your financial situation, something always comes up that wreaks havoc on your budget: a broken washer or refrigerator, a trip to the emergency room, car repairs, the death of a family member or friend, an unexpected shopping spree (think sales and splurges), or even an expected shopping spree (think back-to-school).

You may believe the key to fixing your finances is getting a better-paying job, starting a successful company, or getting a raise. Whatever the option, you know that sooner would be better, because you seem to be sinking fast.

In the rare moments you have time to think seriously about your situation, you also suspect that you or another household member have a spending problem. You are probably thousands of dollars in credit card debt. And while you know that credit card debt is expensive, you feel that there's no way you could stop using them because your checks and auto-pays would almost immediately turn to rubber and start to bounce from bank to bank. Still, you probably don't know exactly how much credit card debt you have on your multiple cards.

You likely do your best to save yourself and your family money by shopping sales and taking advantage of store discounts when you open up store credit cards. You or your spouse may even have tried couponing for a week or two, thinking that might help. Yet each month you realize that you continue to live paycheck to paycheck while those around you appear to be better off than you.

In spite of all of this, you have great hopes for you and your family. You want the best for them and feel you and they deserve more than what you have now.

How do I know this? I also am every man. I know what you're feeling and what you're going through because I've been there, done that. In my younger years, I was not the brightest financial bulb in the box: payday loans, credit card debt settlement, medical collections, maxed out cards (yes, and within thirty-six hours of getting one card), bounced checks. You name it, I've probably done it. While I have not filed for bankruptcy (nor do I have any plans to preach to you about the evils of bankruptcy since those of you thinking that bankruptcy is your only option are most likely right), I've met with thousands of individuals and couples who have. I understand much about the impact of bankruptcy on the individual, the couple, and even the ex-spouse.

Here are a few other likely characteristics I might expect to see in you:

> You have multiple open lines of credit (credit cards, store cards, etc.).

¢ If you own your home, you either owe more than it's worth or have an open line of credit against its equity from which you've borrowed in the past.

¢ You are likely married (or have been married) and are raising children.

¢ You likely carry more than $5,000 of credit card debt from month to month, against which you make only the minimum payments (because paying more would mean that your check or electronic payment would bounce).

¢ You have one checking account.

¢ You have one savings account, but there is never more than $400 or $500 in it. You transfer money over to it every once in a while (maybe $25, $50, or even $100 or more), but always transfer it back to your checking account to keep from bouncing checks (or having to pay overdraft fees).

¢ Your employer probably offers a 401(k) or a 403(b) retirement account option, but you do not have enough money to invest in it.

¢ You've probably started to read a book or two about personal finance but felt they were written for people with a lot more money than you have.

¢ You enjoy dining out but would only be guessing if asked how much you spend at restaurants each year.

¢ You have probably done more than consider playing the lottery. You have either bought a few tickets when the jackpot neared record highs or have purchased tickets each week, hoping to be the "lucky one."

¢ You indulge in some favorite stress relievers: perhaps a morning coffee at the drive-through, a trip to the vending machine each day, a can or two of energy drinks, or a drink on the way home from work.

¢ You are often too worn out at the end of the day to think about making dinner at home (either for yourself or for your family) so stopping at the drive-through or ordering out can seem like a lifesaver.

¢ You owe money on your car loan, or you may even lease your vehicle.

¢ If any (or all) of these situations sound familiar to you, then you're reading the right book. Read on!

Book's Organization

I'm tired of personal finance self-improvement books that look and read like textbooks. Let's be honest. Who loves textbooks? No one! They conjure memories of rote memorization, busy work, and late-night study-a-thons. Nope! Textbooks are not for me, nor, in this case, for you.

I like simple: the simple life, simple flavors, simple games. Some might even say I'm a bit simpleminded, but that's a different book altogether.

Consequently, I've organized my book as more of a handbook and guidebook. In each section, we'll find (1) a brief introduction and overview of the principle or practice on which the section focuses, (2) a story or two to illustrate that principle or practice, (3) a step-by-step checklist of things you ought to consider trying, (4) related quotes, pieces of trivia, or factoids, and (5) a short and straightforward list of Dos and Don'ts to incorporate into everyday finances.

PART ONE

$

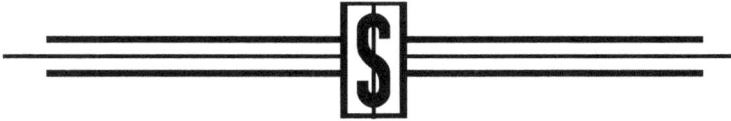

EVERYDAY VALUES

1

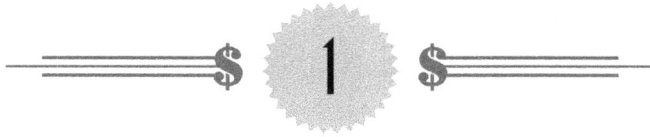

DEFINING YOUR FINANCIAL VISION

I meet people in my classes all the time who have very different visions of what it means to be financially successful. For some, it's an income: "I'm successful because I earn $100,000 a year." For others, it's a lifestyle: "I'm successful because I drive a $70,000 sports car." Still, others tie their financial success to their net worth: "I'm successful because I have a net financial worth in the neighborhood of one million dollars."

These definitions see financial success as a target to shoot for. I define financial success much differently. For me, financial success is a process.

Financial success is simply the extent to which we achieve our financial goals.

When I refer to financial goals, I'm not talking about the big, long-term financial goals, like retirement or buying a home. These are important. However, establishing short-term goals is the best way to get what we want and to stay motivated to live within (or below) our means.

If the only financial goals we have are those that involve thousands (or millions) of dollars and require years or decades of saving to achieve, we will have a near-impossible time staying motivated to achieve those goals. Why? Because we simply do not relate our day-to-day activities, and more importantly, our day-to-day purchases, to large dollar amounts for purposes that are ten or twenty years down the road.

However, if our financial goals are short-term and modest (less than one year away and less than a $1,000), we can easily wrap our minds around both the timeline and size of the goal in order to allow both to influence our daily decisions for the better.

Let's say I'm at work one day, eating soup I brought for lunch (which is pretty common). At some point, I might begin to ask myself if I would prefer to go out for lunch instead. After all, "it's just an extra ten dollars to go to a nice sit-down restaurant where I can enjoy a meal and relax a bit! That ten dollars won't keep me from reaching my $1,000,000 retirement goal, right?" Wrong, actually. It will. Ten dollars a day for thirty years adds up to $108,000. However, invested for thirty years at an average return of 9 percent, that same ten dollars a day will add up to over a half million dollars. So go ahead and enjoy eating out every day for the next thirty years. Just be sure to order a beer to cry in over the $440,000 of lost interest you could have earned.

On the other hand, if my goal is to take a $500 weekend trip to a mountain cabin with my wife five months from now, I quickly understand that each extra ten dollars that I'm spending on dining out makes up a significant portion of my goal . . . two percent in fact. And, being the mathematical wizard that I am, it may only take me the rest of the morning to figure out that I would need to not eat out another fifty times (for two months) in order to equate my savings to the total amount of my goal.

So, setting our own financial goals is the key to achieving financial success. If we still want to set large, long-term goals, then by all means, let's go for it. We just need to break them down into monthly, if not weekly or daily, goals as well.

TODAY'S MONEY

Financial Goals

My wife, Wendy, provides a perfect illustration of this point. Back in 2009, she and I discussed our wish to take our young family on a Disney cruise for a week. Setting aside the discussion of whether a Disney cruise (or any cruise for that matter) is a good idea for a family that included a non-potty-trained one-year old plus a three-year old, let me tell you what that discussion did for us. We determined that we would, after all, take our family on a cruise in the fall of 2010. Once we set that goal, my wife went to work over the next year researching costs for airfare, cruise tickets, hotels, and even passes for an Orlando theme park for a couple of days. Because we had agreed and written that goal down (in our calendars), she was always on the lookout for good deals and certainly found them. She also noticed offers over the next year for special pricing on travel and lodging so that the budget for those expenses amounted to just a fraction of the expected costs.

We ended up spending a wonderful two weeks together, had lots of fun, ate way too much (as all cruisers do), dealt with a few tantrums, made some great memories, had only one broken bone in the family, and were even able to persuade Wendy's mom and her best friend to come along with us (though that didn't take much)—all because Wendy and I turned our "someday wish" into a goal by writing down, looking at, and talking about it frequently.

Step-by-Step Financial Goals

The keys to setting our financial goals involve being specific, keeping them simple, and writing them down.

Having one to three financial goals is a good place to start.

- ¢ First, discuss and write down what you want to purchase or do that will require you to come up with $1,000 or less.

- ¢ Second, determine by what month and year you want to complete or achieve this goal. Don't just write "in six months," because each time you look at your goal, it will still say "in six months." Be specific and write down the month and the year.

- ¢ Third, estimate how much money you will need to save overall in order to reach this goal. Figure out how much that will equate to on a monthly basis.

- ¢ Finally, if you are married, make sure that you involve your spouse in these steps. Having common, mutually agreed-upon financial goals does not guarantee a perfect marriage, but I believe it is the best tip for minimizing arguments about money.

Dos and Don'ts

▲ Do write down a specific goal on a couple of business card-sized pieces of paper.

▲ Do post a goal card on your fridge, nightstand, or bathroom mirror.

▲ Do carry a goal card in your wallet, mixed in with either your cash or your cards, so you are forced to look at your goals each time you make a purchase.

▲ Do read your goals regularly and say them out loud every day or so.

▲ Do consider sharing your goals with those close to you: spouse, parents, siblings, children, best friends, etc. They can encourage us along the way.

▽ Don't rely on wishes alone to motivate you.

▽ Don't seek for riches for riches' sake. Otherwise, your "wishes" for riches amount to nothing more than greed.

▽ Don't argue about money with your spouse. Rather than viewing such arguments as a sign of incompatibility, use this as motivation to set common goals that turn you into financial teammates rather than adversaries.

QUOTE

"Unwritten goals become unfulfilled wishes."

$ 2 $

EASY MONEY? NO. EASY MANAGEMENT? YES.

Wouldn't it be great if money didn't exist at all?

I've heard this many times and, to be honest, thought it myself when I was younger. We say this as if such a solution would solve all of our problems regarding class, want, and need, right? If only we didn't have money, life would be fair and less stressful.

While this line of thinking appears to be the exact opposite of our wish for money to grow on trees (to be ubiquitous), the two actually have much in common.

I think we have these sorts of thoughts most often when money is causing us the most grief. It becomes easy to blame our money problems on money itself. The problem is that those of us who think this way misunderstand the source of money's value. We think that a dollar bill's value is in the one hundred pennies it is worth. We believe the value of a twenty-dollar bill is the pizza we can buy with it.

The true value of money is in the exchange we make, not to spend it but to earn it. Such an exchange can involve effort, ideas, or anything we have that another might desire.

Not convinced? Let's look at the wish for money to grow on trees to illustrate my point. When I visit elementary school classes (which I absolutely love to do) and introduce them to money and finances (earning, spending, saving, etc.), one of the questions I ask is if they would like it if money were to grow on trees. Adults tend to give the same answer, because most of us have never thought much about it. We simply say, "yes," and assume it's a no-brainer. But what if money really did grow on trees? We'd all be better off, right?

Well, if money were to grow on trees (as leaves actually do), here's what I would tell you if you offered me $1,000 just to mow your lawn. "Why would I want your money when I can pull a thousand dollars off a tree any time I want?"

Placing the definition of what we DO with money rather than how we EARN it devalues it in our mind. If we were to always remember that we value money because of what we traded to "get it" (i.e., our time, our energy, our labor, our ideas, etc.), we would likely spend a lot less of it frivolously.

If we figure out that we earn fifteen dollars net per hour at work, and come Saturday morning, we see some doodad on sale somewhere for $150 (half the normal price of $300), we could use the spending-centric point of view to justify the purchase, saying, "Half off is a great deal! After all, I'm saving $150!"

If, on the other hand, we look at the purchase from the earning-centric point of view, we would instead have the following internal conversation, "I had to spend ten hours at work to earn that $150. Is this doodad really worth all the effort I put into working those ten hours?" The doodad may or may not still be worth it, but at least the cost becomes much more personal.

This way of looking at money also has a huge impact on the way we see things such as the lottery, inheritances, and marrying for money. Where there is no effort, there is no perceived value, no appreciation, and no responsibility. Would this explain why such a high percentage of children who receive regular financial gifts from their affluent parents end up having dramatically lower net worths compared to those who receive no such gifts from affluent parents?[1] Or those who win $50,000 to $150,000 in state lotteries and end up filing for bankruptcy at the same rate as those who win less than $10,000?[2] Even multimillion-dollar lottery winners can slip into the financial abyss.

Not dissimilarly, the rate of personal bankruptcies and financial stress among recently retired NFL players is an astounding 78 percent.[3] Many of these individuals who "played" their way to multimillion-dollar contracts could overnight afford to live the high life (and often did), and then, when the knee gave out or the ankle didn't heal, found it virtually impossible to adjust to living on less or, at the very least, change their way of viewing money and investments. I'm not suggesting that they didn't work hard. I know my measly two weeks of two-a-day high school football practices in 110° heat didn't compare to what the professionals go through, and those just about killed me. But it's no difficult argument to make that many of our professional athletes and celebrities are overpaid with relation to the effort and time put into developing their profession. The same could be said about young, overnight, millionaire entrepreneurs. Not all of these usually young and exorbitantly paid individuals lack appreciation for their income. Many do appreciate their wealth, and those who do, tend to be less visible to us since they often shun the lavish lifestyles, expensive cars, and top-of-the-line, must-have, currently trendy clothing.

At this point, some are probably asking, "Why such an emphasis, Todd, on the vice of easy money?" The easy answer, in the immortal words of parents worldwide: "because!"

I know that I'm making it sound like having loads of money is a curse, and many of us would quickly say, "May I be cursed with such a curse! In fact, make it a double!" It's not the money that is the problem, or even the actual method of obtaining it. It's the likelihood that those who seek easy money tend to be those who least appreciate its value.

Seriously.

Because easy money does not solve our problems. If we don't properly value our meager or modest incomes right now, we likely don't manage it responsibly, and throwing more money at the problem will never fix it. Take the federal government as a case study there.

So I'm finally getting around to the issue of making money management a less stressful part of your life. You want to make managing your money easier, because, after all, you typically put a lot of sweat, effort, and time into earning it. Too many financial experts, however, propose elaborate systems for managing money. After all, aren't financial experts right when they say, "The more time you spend with your money, the more details you can understand and control about your finances, the better off you'll be"? It's a pretty common sentiment. I may have even said such things years and years ago. But I was wrong to say them. I apologize. I'm sorry. Please forgive me. It is now very much my solid belief that you should make money management tasks boring, predictable, simple, and foolproof.

Here's what I'm proposing throughout this book: make money management easy. I'll show you how to eliminate decisions related to many of your daily, weekly, monthly, annual, and even period financial purchases, along with the stress that tends to accompany them. By keeping the true value of your money in mind, you will actually tend to automatically spend less, collect less debt, and save and invest more. By eliminating as many decisions about money as you can, its management becomes easier, even routine. And when it comes to managing money, I'm all for boring.

TODAY'S MONEY

Easy Money Story

The sooner we stop wishing for money to magically appear in our checking account, the more likely we are to become productive contributors to our communities and society in general.

Big media loves to fan the flames of lottery lust and to hype big winners. I just wish they equally covered the lives of those winners five to ten years later. While many big lottery winners successfully manage their newly gained nonearnings, it's not difficult to find story after story of past winners (from many countries) now in bankruptcy or on welfare.[4]

I find the story of Michael Carroll, a $15,000,000 (9.7 million pounds in Britain) winner in 2002 a perfect illustration for this chapter, and not because of his uncommon situation. It's actually not. Less than a decade after cashing his winning check, he was broke and unemployed. What fascinates me most is the clarity of how he summed up his current financial situation: "That's the way I like it. I find it easier to live off £42 dole than a million."[5]

What he said is that it was easy for him to collect and live off of $65 in unemployment than to manage millions of dollars. If we have trouble managing a meager or modest income, what makes us think we'll be able to manage a million dollars?

Step-by-Step Easy Money Management

Understanding the True Value of Money

- ¢ First of all, let's determine your net pay per hour. Simply divide the dollar amount of your paycheck by the number of hours you worked to earn it. For example, if your paycheck were $1,200, and you worked eighty hours (two weeks) to get it, your net pay is fifteen dollars/hour ($1,200 ÷ 80 = $15).

- ¢ Next, in order to figure out the true value of a ten-dollar bill, a $120 purchase, or a $15,000 car loan, divide the amount by your net hourly pay. If your net hourly pay is fifteen dollars, then to earn a ten-dollar bill, you need to work for forty minutes ($10 ÷ $15/hour = 2/3 hour or 40 minutes). To earn enough money to make a $120 purchase, you must spend an entire day at work ($120 ÷ $15/hour = 8 hours). If you were to borrow $15,000 for a car, first remember you'll end up paying a total of $16,875 at 5 percent interest over the next five years. That means you will have to work 141 days (six and a half months of work) just to pay for that vehicle. Is that car worth working an additional half year or more just to pay it off?

Dos and Don'ts

▲ Do determine your true net hourly income.

▲ Do figure out how many hours and days of work you need to put in to earn $10, $100, $1,000, and $10,000.

▲ Do learn to appreciate the "penny earned" part of Benjamin Franklin's famous quote, and not just the "penny saved" phrase.

▽ Don't waste a single dollar on lottery tickets.

▽ Don't waste your time and energy waiting for easy money to happen to you. Make it happen yourself.

EASY MONEY INSIGHT

NFL star Raghib (Rocket) Ismail describes wonderfully what many of us, not just professional athletes, experience when we first attempt to learn about investing: "I once had a meeting with J. P. Morgan, and it was literally like listening to Charlie Brown's teacher."[6] When money seems plentiful and easy to come by, we can quickly turn off the "whaa whaa whaa" of the money "teacher," considering it unnecessary, at least for the moment.

CREATING FINANCIAL HOPE AND OPPORTUNITIES

Hope cannot be manufactured. Hope must come from within. When hope is missing in life, the future appears dark and menacing. In my classes, I often meet people who feel financially hopeless, having lost job after job, using up any emergency savings they had, feeling as though no matter what they do, it will never be enough to overcome their challenges.

Then, there are others who sit right next to the hopeless, who have gone and are going through very similar challenges, and yet remain hopeful for a positive future. How is it that they remain so? Does hope matter? Do the hopeful end up more financially successful than the hopeless?

I know, some are thinking right now, "no duh," and according to the gospel of Todd, hope is vital to financial success. By financial success, I'm not talking about earning a certain income or saving a certain amount or living a certain lifestyle. I'm referring to achieving one's financial goals. Without hope, we may feel that all is lost and that no matter what we do, our financial lives and financial futures are predestined toward failure. Consequently, we stop looking for opportunities to progress, and stop taking advantage of situations that would lead us to an improved future.

With hope, on the other hand, we believe that our future will be better than our present. We stay alert and make ourselves aware of what is going on around us that can benefit us.

The hopeless think that hope is a feeling.

The hopeful know that hope is an action.

So, what action or actions should the financially hopeless take in order to become the financially hopeful?

Let me answer by sharing the experience I continue to have regularly in my classes. When I walk into a class, I can tell within a matter of minutes who is or eventually will be financially successful. It's not discerned by the clothing they wear, the watches or jewelry they're sporting, their accent, or the color of their skin. Those who are or will eventually be financially successful are those who are actively involved in the presentation. Whether the class I'm teaching is their first experience in financial education or they already have an MBA, those who are or will be financially successful are those who are open to continued learning. The main group of class attendees I truly worry about are those individuals sitting in the back, arms folded, glaring at me with an expression that seems to say, "I dare you to teach me something because I'm not interested," or "There's nothing you're saying that is of interest to me because I already know all of this."

I've been studying, researching, and teaching these topics for almost a decade now and still learn something new virtually every week. Since I'm not a remarkable person, I'm sure that if I can learn something new, others can too.

The goal of this section is not that you learn something new, but that you, especially if you're lacking it, build hope for your financial future.

What can you do to build that hope? I'm not guaranteeing that your dreams will come true, but your main task is to envision the kind of financial future you desire and simply write it down.

No one will be surprised that I didn't get too far into this book without saying something about financial goals, right? Well, as expected, here we are, still in Part I, and I'm bringing up the annoying financial goals bit already. Isn't a goals-writing exercise just fluff, meant to kill time and fill workbooks sold by financial experts? No. It's actually important because it works.

Here's what I do in many of my classes: I ask what types of financial goals most of us have either set for ourselves or have at least heard about. The top two answers I get, in a virtual dead heat, are (1) retire well and (2) buy a home. Why are these essentially the only financial goals we come up with? Because there's money to be had in helping people reach these goals, and if that's the case, there are businesses set up to help, and these businesses tend to advertise.

We hear of them because a business is selling them to us. That's not a bad thing. These goals are both worthy and important. But for most of the financially hopeless, both of these goals are too long term in scope and too large in breadth. Here's the problem, mathematically speaking:

$$\text{Financial Goal Motivation} = 1/(\$ \times \text{time period})$$

Before calling me a geek or a nerd for converting financial goals into a math equation (too late, I'm sure), here's what this problem means in plain English and why it's important.

The more money we have invested into our goal and the longer the time period we have to reach it, the less motivation the goal provides us.

Why? Because we are creatures of the present. We don't live in the future. Our reality is today and possibly a few days or weeks down the road. Setting a goal, for example, to have $1,000,000 in retirement investments thirty years from now is something to which we just can't relate in our daily decision making. Seriously! What does $1,000,000 have to do with whether I'm going out for a fifteen-dollar dinner tonight? A lot, when we think about it. But since most of us, off the top of our head, would be hard pressed to figure out, first, how many fifteen-dollar dinners we could enjoy with $1,000,000 (66,667ish, in case you're wondering), and, second, we have no concept of how many dinners that really is (is that a lifetime's worth, two lifetimes, or more? Actually, it's 182 years worth), there is no emotional connection between the fifteen-dollar expense and the $1,000,000 goal. Without that emotional connection, there is no braking system to keep spending from speeding out of control and over a financial cliff.

I believe the most motivating goals we can set for ourselves are the small short-term ones (I know, that one struck like a bolt out of right field—yes, I love mixed-up metaphors). I'm talking about things we want to buy, activities we want to do, achievements we want to, well, achieve, and savings we want to build within the next six to twelve months and require less than $1,000.

Once we have these small, short-term goals written down, we have established a vision of our future *and* a path for getting there. If we can set up these expectations for what we want in the future, we've just given ourselves some financial hope. I think a congratulatory pat on the back is appropriate at the moment. Go ahead, no one's looking.

Now that we've got some financial hope in place, what about some financial faith and charity? Well, thanks for asking. Keep reading for more about charity, and have faith that we'll find additional ideas for improving our financial future.

Financial Hope and Opportunity

Here's how goal setting really works. It's not that writing a goal will somehow magically give us more income to achieve that goal. Rather, by writing down our goals, we're more likely to notice opportunities to achieve them. Here's the example I use in my classes:

Let's say my wife, Wendy, and I, sometime in the next six months, want to go on a three-day romantic getaway to our country's first ski resort (that would be Sun Valley, here in Idaho). Once we write that wish down, it then becomes a goal.

Since we've written it down and posted it somewhere that's visible to us each day, we'll be on the lookout for opportunities to go to Sun Valley. Here's how the magic works:

Imagine a conversation with a friend who says he just returned from a trip to Sun Valley, a perfect weekend. If Wendy and I hadn't written down the goal, the conversation with him would probably end with the words, "That's great! I'm glad you had a good time." That's it.

But since we wrote down the goal, when I hear my friend mention Sun Valley, I'm all over it.

"Where did you stay? What did you do? Any recommendations?" It might come out that my friend stayed at his sister's condo in Sun Valley, and that she's more than happy to cut us a fantastic deal for our three-day getaway.

Writing down goals doesn't make them magically happen. It does, however, make us absolutely more aware of opportunities that come our way that will help us to achieve our goal.

TODAY'S MONEY

Financial Hope and Opportunity Step-by-Step

You may have heard of SMART goals. While there is a traditional version of SMART goals taught the world over, I'll use the following modified version: Specific, Meaningful, Attainable, Rewarding, and Timely. Let's follow these steps to create powerful, personal finance goals:

¢ Specific: Write down what you want to do, buy, or achieve. Include details that answer questions such as, "Who is involved?" and "Where is this activity or product?"

¢ Meaningful: Whatever you choose to write down as a goal had better be important to you. It can be a vacation to the beach, a picnic in the mountains, or a set of new tires for your Hyundai. As long as it's important to you, it will be motivational, and you'll be more likely to stick with it.

¢ Attainable: Keep the amount of money required for this goal fairly modest, usually requiring $1,000 or less. If the amount gets to be too much more than that, you're less likely to see it as a realistic goal.

¢ Rewarding: Imagine yourself achieving the goal. Write down a few words or phrases that you believe will describe how you'll feel. You might write down something like, "I'll be walking on Cloud Nine, having fulfilled a life-long dream." Hopefully that's not what follows the "Buy a new set of tires for the Hyundai" goal. Or, you might write, "I'll finally feel a weight lifted from my shoulders when I remove this goal from my to-do list." Give this step the time it merits. Really consider the reason you want to achieve it and spell it out.

¢ Timely: Write down the month and year in which you want to achieve this goal. Writing "six months from now" doesn't cut it. Every time you look at the goal in the future, it will still tell you that you have another six months. That's not good enough. Write down the month and the year you want to accomplish the goal, and make sure it's not more than twelve months away. Beyond twelve months, for most of us, time becomes a bit too nebulous. It becomes too easy to see that much time as "plenty of time." Time in which to do what? To procrastinate, that's what. When you make the time frame short term, you're more likely to go to work on it immediately.

Dos and Don'ts

▲ Do write the goal down (typed or handwritten is fine too).

▲ Do post the goal where it will be visible regularly (bathroom mirror, refrigerator, nightstand, or as a card in your wallet or purse).

▲ Do share your goals with others. If married, sharing with your spouse should be a no-brainer. You may also consider sharing on social media with friends to garner their support and encouragement.

▽ Don't overreach.

▽ Don't see your goal as inflexible. If your values and your goals change, that's okay. Rewrite them.

▽ Don't give up.

QUOTE

"A written goal turns fantasy into reality."
—Student in my May 2013 budgeting class

PART TWO

$

EVERYDAY GIVING

GIVING MEANS GETTING

Giving comes in many shapes and sizes. For the purposes of this book, I'm not talking exclusively about donating certain sums of money. Everyone has something to give. If we have the capacity to read and reason, we have something to give. It might be money, a talent, our time, our efforts, or our ideas.

Regardless of *what* we give, I truly believe that generously giving is the first step to financial stability and success for a variety of reasons:

¢ First, giving forces us to consider that we do not achieve financial stability or success independent of others. We can't *earn* money without others being willing to pay us something of value in exchange. Giving, then, leads us to work with and appreciate others, without whom we cannot be successful.

¢ Giving also helps us to recognize the needs of others and to appreciate what we have. With such appreciation often comes a partial or complete rejection of the frivolous, the trivial, and the trendy. Additionally, understanding the needs of others is the key to entrepreneurial success. Our professional mantra becomes, "See a need; fill a need."

¢ However, giving away our money does not mean that we'll become financially wealthy. Although for the large number of potential entrepreneurs among us, awareness of the needs of others can directly lead to solutions that our society values and is willing to pay for.

¢ Finally, when we give, whether we do so openly or anonymously, I truly believe good things will happen to us. Whether you see this as karma or as the fulfillment of the truth found in Ecclesiastes 11:1, "Cast thy bread upon the waters: for thou shalt find it after many days," or whether you just believe that good things happen to good people, I believe you're right.

From a financial perspective, the more generous we are with our time, talents, resources, and everything we've been blessed with, the more likely we are to understand how the economic and social systems work to our advantage and to our disadvantage. We become more aware of human services programs that help those in need and that, heaven forbid, we might have to take advantage of ourselves someday.

At this point, I'm sure that some of you are thinking, "Of course I'd be more generous, if only I had more money." Interestingly, most of today's millionaires were raising funds for good causes before they became financially independent, and most did it because of noble intent. For whatever the reason, givers are prone to being not just "getters" but the "getters ahead" in this life. After all, most financially successful and stable individuals in this country are extraordinarily active, busy people who dedicate their lives not to amassing wealth for wealth's sake, but to their work or business with the purpose of fulfilling or meeting the needs of others.

I am not promising, of course, that if you give away your money and possessions to those in need that you will end up better off financially. Rather, I strongly encourage each one of you to make giving an integral part of your monthly finances and part of your monthly living. As you make the commitment to give to worthy causes that help others, my belief is that you will be better stewards or managers of the income and assets you already have.

There is just something special about being generous. There really is. It goes contrary to many a long-held practice (if not belief) that wealth comes through saving and amassing and collecting rather than through giving away.

CHAPTER 4: GIVING MEANS GETTING

Generosity first. Wealth next.

I truly believe and have experienced that giving a portion of our income, whether through donations or tithes, strongly impacts our finances for the best. In addition to tithing's component of faith, the mere practice of giving away a portion of our income is a way of definitively stating that we do not exist or live in a void, that you and I are fellow travelers on life's journey, and that we both depend upon and feel responsible for each other's success. It is partially this life view that, I believe, leads us to long-term financial success. By taking care of others (however we choose to define or understand that phrase), we consequently become aware of others who might have something that we need, whether it be food and clothing or business and professional advice.

I like to define this personality trait as humility (which I also think of as "being teachable"). Being humble allows us to learn and grow and progress throughout our lives. When I'm teaching a class, no matter how little or how much individuals in the group know and understand about finances, the only ones I really worry about are those who sit back with their arms folded across their chest looking like they already know everything about finances that there is to know.

I've been studying, learning, and teaching personal finance for nearly a decade, facilitating nearly a thousand classes to thousands upon thousands of individuals and conference goers, yet I still learn something new pretty much every week about managing my money. So when I read and learn that those who are among the most financially successful have been extra generous throughout their lives, that's a lesson we all should learn ourselves, and if we want to experience financial success, we should determine to give.

How much? I like the idea of actually giving beyond what we think is easy to give.

TODAY'S MONEY

Parable of the Three Teenagers

Three teenaged friends enjoyed being selfless.

The first teenager liked to pay the bridge toll for unknown drivers behind him.

The second teenager gave money and bottles of water to those asking for help on street corners.

The third teenager gave discreetly to his church and to charities of his choice.

Which of the three teenagers should receive the greater reward?

If that's the question you're asking, then you need to readjust your thinking. All three did something noble and worthwhile with their giving. It is not for us to judge which is more worthwhile. It is only up to us to do our best at emulating one or more of them. We should give to do good, not because we expect to benefit from it.

Step-by-Step

If you're not a natural giver (and there are many who aren't), consider putting your philanthropy on autopilot. Reflect on the following steps:

1. Accept that automating your giving does not cheapen it.
2. Determine the amount that you can afford to give regularly.
3. Consider increasing that amount by 5 or 10 percent or more.
4. Set up an automatic contribution using your bank or credit union's free online bill pay or by setting up an automatic withdrawal directly through the beneficiary.

FACTOID

According to a recent Giving USA annual report, individuals in the United States gave a total of about $218 billion dollars to churches and charities in 2011. With about 117 million households in the United States (according to the US Census Bureau), this means that the average household donates approximately $1,863 to churches and charities each year.

Dos and Don'ts

▲ Do choose a nonprofit charity or church to which you donate monthly, whether the amount is $5 or $500.

▲ Do add an additional amount to your spending plan that you can give away spontaneously.

▲ Do give more than just money. Give time, heart, skills, and compassion.

▽ Don't flaunt what or how much you give.

▽ Don't belittle or discount the philanthropy of others.

▽ Don't give because you expect to get.

5

GIVE WHERE YOUR MONEY MEETS YOUR VALUES

In my home state of Idaho alone, there are over two thousand non-profit charitable organizations. Two thousand! I guarantee each one of them would accept our financial contribution if we offered it. (*Disclosure: I am employed by one of those 2,000 nonprofit charitable organizations and have been a volunteer board member for another, so although I give my opinion on the subject, take what I say as coming from an insider.*)

The next question, then, becomes the following: to which of all of the possible organizations out there should we donate our hard-earned money?

Many of us have probably read blogs or articles that suggest first checking with databases that track nonprofit charities to identify the most "efficient" nonprofits. This argument makes the assumption that the lower the overhead (meaning the less the nonprofit spends on administrative costs such as salaries, rent, equipment, and supplies), the more the nonprofit will spend on the direct service to those who benefit from the program. I understand the logic of this approach, although I don't completely agree with the assumption. This line of reasoning, if carried to the extreme, would place at the top of the list an all-volunteer charity with no physical place of business, no copy machines, and no pencils or pens for the volunteers to use. Clearly, overhead should not be the sole, or the most important, consideration when determining where to donate.

In fact, even before considering a list of the nonprofit charities registered within our state (such as the IRS's Select Check at www.irs. gov/Charities-&-Non-Profits/Exempt-Organizations-Select-Check and www.NonProfitList.org), I suggest that you first make a list of your personal values that might impact your choice (see Step-by-Step in next section). If you're married, make sure to include your spouse in this decision.

The next question to be asked would be regarding how much to give. How much is enough? Of course, this is a personal decision (or one between spouses), but let me share my own thoughts.

First, when it comes to tithes, it might help to understand that the origin of the word means one-tenth. It's up to each of us to answer, "One-tenth of what?" Gross income, net income, net worth increase over the previous year, or other?

For any donation, though, when it comes to how much to give, here's my rule:

Give an amount that you're comfortable with . . . and then give at least a little more.

If only giving out of our abundance, there is no personal sacrifice or investment in it. We won't miss the money and may care little about how it's used. However, if we give a greater amount than we are comfortable giving, we will then have an emotional tie to it and to the recipients. We're likely to do more than just give. We'll be more likely to get involved in the cause as well, and the more involved we are, the more satisfaction and joy we will derive from it.

When it comes to giving, it's okay to be a little uncomfortable.

TODAY'S MONEY

Give Where Your Money Meets Your Values

I recently attended a conference of nonprofit credit counseling agencies, held in the fabulous city of San Antonio, Texas. One of the speakers shared a story that shocked both her and her colleagues at a consumer rights organization. She told of a nonprofit that catered to individuals looking for assistance to pay off their overwhelming debts. This nonprofit would often charge more than a thousand dollars to "qualify" the individuals for a debt management program before referring them to another nonprofit debt counseling agency that then provided the actual service. In essence, the thousand dollars functioned as a referral fee for the organization.

If the speaker was shocked, we, as credit counseling professionals, were dumbfounded (seriously, the hotel staff almost had to jimmy rig supports to prop up our jaws by the end of the story). Bad apples in our industry from early in the 2000s ended up in jail because of such unprincipled and downright greedy policies.

Moral of the story? Just because the Internal Revenue Service classifies an organization as a nonprofit (1) does not mean it is "no profit" and (2) certainly does not guarantee that such an organization provides a needed or even beneficial service to its community and customers. It's easy to find illustrations by simply googling, "nonprofit scandals."

Give Where Our Money Meets Our Values Step-by-Step

One question you need to answer when determining to which organization you should donate is this:

1. What are the deficiencies in society that you would most want to see addressed? Answers might include poverty, illiteracy, homelessness, domestic violence, crime, child abuse, drug abuse, civil or human rights violation, or animal cruelty, just to name a few.

    On the flip side, you could also ask this question:

2. What are the most important things to you individually, as a society, or nation? Your list might include your faith, your family relationships, education, research, or health.

    Next, apply demographic filters to your answers, narrowing them by the age of those you'd like to serve (the unborn, infants, toddlers, children, youth, young adults, adults, seniors), their economic status (unemployed, low income, low-to-moderate income, etc.), their geographic scope (hyper-local, local, state, regional, national, international), faith, political persuasion, education level, race or ethnicity, and so forth.

3. With this list in hand, you can now consider your list of non-profit charities and begin to eliminate those worthy as they may be, which do not address the core values you've just identified or that do not serve the populations you seek to help.

    As you approach giving in this way, remember that you will still be frequently solicited by multiple organizations that would like you to donate your resources. Individually, we cannot give to everyone. We have to be prepared to say no. For me, I find that when it comes to any difficult decision, it's easier if I know ahead of time what my choice is and what my response will be. So the next time someone asks us to donate to a cause that is not on our giving list, we can use a phrase like, "What a great cause! I'd like to know more about it so I can consider it the next time I'm ready to donate," or simply, "No, thank you, but I wish you all the best."

4. If you truly like the cause or organization that is soliciting you for money you haven't planned to donate to, and if it will make you feel better (and it often will), offer to help promote it on your Facebook, Twitter, or other social media pages to help spread the word about the good they are doing.

5. One other possible suggestion would be to carry around a small amount of cash for just such occasions. It might be five dollars a month or it could be fifty dollars, depending upon your budget. Think of this money as belonging to someone else, and that you're only caring for it until you find the best service organization to be a steward of it. One month, you might choose to give this money to the Salvation Army's bell ringers. Another month, the Girls Scouts may be the happy recipients of your donation (and you the happy recipients of a box of Thin Mints® or Samoas®). Other months, you may find it rewarding to give a few dollars to someone (whether or not you know them) who is down on their luck. Giving directly can provide you with a positive and uplifting feeling that the budgeted and planned giving may not. Enjoy it!

FACTOID

Religious organizations receive the largest portion of our donations in this country, at thirty-two cents of every dollar given.[1] Next on the list of recipients, right around thirteen cents of every dollar given, is the educational sector, including colleges and universities, public and private K–12 schools, and organizations promoting and supporting educational programs.

Dos and Don'ts

When deciding upon a beneficiary of our donations . . .

▲ Do find them on the IRS website of nonprofits.

▲ Do research them at www.bbb.org.

▲ Do remember you can't give to every good cause that solicits a donation.

▽ Don't make your donation decisions based solely on giving to the charity with the lowest percentage of expenses going to overhead costs.

▽ Don't forget to research charities at CharityNavigator.com and other websites before donating to them.

▽ Don't compare your philanthropy with that of others. Let others give what they can, and be grateful for what you have to offer.

PART THREE

$

EVERYDAY PAYCHECK PLANNING

TURNING YOUR BUDGET FROM FOE TO FRENEMY

When I ask my classes what percentage of their fellow citizens they think are living paycheck to paycheck, the typical first responses are in the 80–90 percent range. Consequently, when I share that the most recent survey from the Financial Industry Regulatory Authority Inc. (www.usfinancialcapability.org) indicates that only 40 percent of us are living paycheck to paycheck, they're usually pleasantly surprised.

Then, of course, I burst their bubble of optimism about our collective financial responsibility by noting that another 20 percent of the population actually spends more than what they earn each month. All in all, 60 percent of the households in America (that's sixty-nine million American households) and the approximately 188 million American men, women, and children living in them spend every penny or more of what they regularly earn.

There are endless reasons for why we don't live by a budget: too many bills, downsizing, banks charge excessive interest, the kids and the ex-spouse take all of the money, the government collects too much in taxes, it's too stressful, we don't know how, and so forth. In fact, just this week, I asked a class to create a list of why more people don't live by a budget, and their list included all of these reasons just listed. I'm also aware of the following excuses:

"I don't make enough money to budget."

If this is our excuse, then we will always feel like we're poor, no matter how much we earn now or in the future.

"I make so much money, I don't need a budget."

It is human nature that the more money we earn, the more we spend. Is it any wonder that formerly high-paid professional athletes who never erected the purchase constraints so vital to long term financial stability are financially stressed or bankrupt within just two or three years of retirement?[1] There is no such thing as having so much money that it doesn't need to be managed wisely.

"I can never do anything fun on a budget."

Many of us who feel this way have tried budgets before and probably found that, in spite of putting aside money each month for movies, concerts, dates, or other planned-for events, we could never be spontaneous. This is a common result of trying to plan for every activity and event. The problem is that we can't possibly plan for everything that will come up in the next thirty days. That's why many personal finance experts, myself included, suggest incorporating a specified amount of money into our budgets that can be spent at anytime on anything during the month. This money is for splurges and spontaneity. It might be five dollars a month if money's tight. It might be one hundred dollars or more if our situation allows it. Regardless of the amount, it allows us to live by a budget, while also helping us to be prepared for moments of spontaneity.

"I don't have time to budget!"

Tackling a household budget can, admittedly, be more than a bit daunting. In what one of my former financial educators called a "financial huddle," which are short, weekly budgeting sessions, you can increase your understanding of what's going on financially in your household, build greater control over your expenses, and decrease the stress so often imbedded in household finances.

Here are the four simple steps of a fifteen-minute, weekly financial huddle: (1) At the same time on the same day every week, pull out your list of short-term goals, (2) balance your checkbook, (3) look ahead seven to ten days and figure out what bills need to be paid, how you'll pay them (check, cash, bill pay, by mail, in person, etc.), and (4) return to your goals and figure out what to do in the upcoming week to get closer to reaching those goals. One hour a month is an amount of time we can all carve out of our schedules.

I hear these and other excuses all too often. But, like one of my high school coaches told me, "You can give me reasons, but there are no excuses." Listing excuse after excuse to justify why we live paycheck to paycheck, rather than planning our expenses and savings, leads us right into the victim mentality that will forever keep us from making important decisions that lead to real progress. It will not be until we tell ourselves (and we believe it) that our financial destiny truly is our own to choose and create that we will begin to make great strides towards success.

There are plenty of reasons why we think our situation is unique and plenty of explanations as to why a budget will not help us. For most of us with excuses for not budgeting, we think of budgets as forms to fill out or numbers to crunch. Please, please, please, let's destroy this idea of a budget once and for all.

A budget is not a form. It is not an exercise. Budgets are simply tools that come in various makes and models, and they allow us to erect spending barriers against unnecessary and unimportant consumer purchases in our lives, while channeling our income into what we have identified as truly important.

So let's change our budgets from foes to, if not friends, at least frenemies.

Enough excuses! Read on, implement, repeat, succeed!

TODAY'S MONEY

Foe to Frenemy

I have sometimes heard students repine that if they only made more money, they wouldn't need to bother with budgets. Many of us as adults think this way as well. "If I only had a million dollars, all my financial worries would be over." Wrong!

What would we do with a million dollars? Well, if we're not on a budget, we'd almost certainly spend it and spend it in a hurry.

When I go into middle school classes, I love to ask the question, "How would you spend $100,000 by the end of the week?" And guess what? The students come up with numerous ways to dump $100,000 in just a few days. If they can do it, so can we, especially if we don't curb our spending by budgeting.

Budgets are all about controlling our spending sprees that are lurking just under the surface. It's time we show budgets the respect and the appreciation they deserve, and the best way to do that is to use them.

Step-by-Step Foe to Frenemy

¢ Choose a time and day of the week to hold a weekly financial huddle.

¢ Review your week's successes and failures at the next huddle (and report them to your spouse if you're married).

¢ If you want a simplified spending plan, consider the 10-10-20-60 budget: 10 percent of your net income goes to others in the form of donations, 10 percent goes to long-term planning, 20 percent goes to short-term savings (emergency fund, appliances and furniture, holiday gift giving, vacation, etc.), and 60 percent goes to all living expenses (housing, groceries, bills, etc.).

FINANCIAL FACTOID

According to the *2012 Consumer Literacy Survey* prepared by Harris Interactive, a mere 43 percent of American adults have a budget and track their expenditures regularly.

Dos and Don'ts

▲ Do commit in writing to yourself and to your spouse (if you're married) to hold a weekly financial huddle.

▲ Do keep your budgets tied directly to short-term goals.

▲ Do continue to balance regularly any checking account(s) you have.

▽ Don't make your budgets too complex.

▽ Don't estimate your total expenses before prioritizing them.

▽ Don't give up. A practical and working budget can take six months or more to develop and hone.

7

TAKING THE EXCITEMENT OUT OF YOUR FINANCES

Those of us hoping that this book will provide some new, exciting method or trick to manage our finances are likely to be disappointed. As it so happens, I'm a believer in boring finances, and the more boring the better. If our finances are exciting, that means they're unpredictable and full of surprises and drama. Isn't life itself already thrilling enough? Our finances need not be dramatic. That's why the key to making our finances boring is to "fix" them. And by "fix," I mean to set them in place and in routine, not repair, although that is also a result.

Back in the late 2005, I wrote a booklet for individuals and couples who file for bankruptcy. As many readers of this book likely know, those filing bankruptcy are required to take a two-hour debtor education course prior to the court discharging them of their legal responsibility to repay debts. The booklet I wrote, *Making Good Sense of Bankruptcy*, has since formed the basis of hundreds of classes Debt Reduction Services, Inc. has taught to thousands of bankruptcy filers.

One of the activities we do in these classes is to survey the students about their situation. I ask them, among other things, to identify the cause or origin of their financial crisis. When I ask my nonbankruptcy classes to guess the bankruptcy filer's top responses to this question, typical answers include, "They got into a house they couldn't afford," or "They couldn't pay their medical bills." Such answers likely stem from all of the media attention given to the housing market and the high costs associated with our health care system.

However, in all of the surveys we've gathered, not one of them has ever identified their home as being too large for their budget. While it's quite likely that many were living in homes that were too big for their income level, they never identified their homes as the cause of bankruptcy. The top answers, in order, have been: (1) job loss or income reduction, (2) poor money management habits and over-spending, (3) medical bills, and (4) divorce. My point here is that even though our mortgage or rent is likely the largest expense in our household budgets, we tend to figure out a way to make the payment month after month. In fact, such fixed payments (same amount every month) are among the easiest to manage, in spite of being some of the largest in our budgets. Besides housing, other fixed expenses include car payments, insurance premiums, and contracted services (Internet, cell phone, etc.). Why are they easy to pay? Because they're boring. They're fixed and fixed expenses just get paid. We prepare for them and save for them throughout the month, even if only subconsciously, because they become routine.

Conversely, the more our monthly bills vary or the more periodic they are in nature, the more trouble they cause us. That's why utilities, gasoline, groceries, dining out, and gift giving become such financial headaches for so many individuals and families. The amount we spend on them always varies, so how are we supposed to budget for them or actually stick to the budgeted amount? For many, this seems like nothing more than a guessing game.

Let's make this easy on us. Remember, I'm all about boring and predictable budgets. Let our excitement in life come from living, not budgeting.

There are several options available that can turn variable and periodic expenses into monthly expenses that are fixed. In this way, we get rid of the financial surprises that all too often lead to increasing credit card debt, defaulting on loans, or seeking out highly expensive borrowing options such as payday, title, or pawn loans.

First, the easiest of these variable monthly expenses to fix are the household utilities bills. Who hasn't received their heating bill in January or February and started sweating in the cold winter weather, trying to figure out just how to pay a bill two or three times higher than it was just a few months earlier? Well, the good news is that there's an easy way to turn this variable monthly expense into a predictable and boring one. Simply call your electric company (most heating companies offer this as well) and ask them to put you on their "level pay" program. Some call it by other names, but the idea is the same. The electric company looks back at your previous twelve months of bills, takes their average, and bills you that amount each month going forward. Simple as that. Your utility bills are now fixed. No more surprises. No more headaches. Yes, your summer heating bill will be a little more expensive than it used to be, but your winter heating bill will be a lot less than it was.

The real benefit of these programs is the predictability of monthly bills. It makes it infinitely easier to plan utility payments when you're on such programs.

But what about groceries, some might ask? Has anyone ever called the local grocery store or supermarket and asked to get on their level pay? Wouldn't that be nice? "I'll just come in and get whatever I need whenever I need it and send you the same payment at the end of each month."

Unfortunately, that's unlikely to happen, although if it ever does, would someone please let me know?

Still, you can always put your household on your own fixed grocery plan. It's a lot simpler than might be expected. Here are at least three good options:

¢ Consider opening up a second checking account at the same bank or credit union you currently work with (if you don't have an account at a bank or credit union due to a "poor" experience in the past, I suggest that you consider looking for a "BankOn" program nearby—joinbankon.org/programs—or ask around for a "Second Chance Checking" account). I would suggest that you *never* open up a second checking account if your financial institution requires a monthly fee for it. There are other options that are cheaper. Once you have a second checking account, set up an automatic transfer from your main checking account into this new groceries account (every week, every two weeks, or every month) for the amount you have planned just for groceries. Next, use a debit card, checks, or cash withdrawals from this grocery account to purchase groceries. Oh, and leave your debit card and checks from your main account at home when you go shopping, so you're not tempted to use them when going over your planned purchases at the grocery store. If you're tempted to continually transfer money from your main account into the grocery account because it's an easy way to cover impulse expenses at the grocery store or supermarket, consider opening the grocery account at a bank or credit union separate from the one where your main checking account is located. That will make it more difficult and inconvenient to transfer money back and forth to cover such expenses and, as a result, keep you more motivated to spend only what's in your grocery account.

NOTE: Consider including not only grocery expenses in this account but also any expenses typically from the store where you purchase the groceries. For example, if you shop at a supermarket where you buy cleaning supplies, sporting equipment, DVDs, clothing, in addition to groceries, your spending plan will be based not on what you shop for but where you shop.

¢   If you choose not to have a checking account or still can't qualify for one at the moment, consider purchasing a gift card from the store or supermarket where you do your grocery shopping. Many gift cards may have a purchase or activation fee, so be sure that the card you use does not. Other fees to avoid include loading and reloading fees, monthly fees, and account closure fees.

NOTE: Please be aware that I'm not talking here about gift cards with the Visa, MasterCard, Discover, or American Express card logos. Such cards typically have higher activation fees, plus they are too flexible for your purposes. If they can be spent just about anywhere, then that's missing the point. You want a card that is only good at the store where you're purchasing groceries.

¢   The third and final option has a few fees associated with it, but those fees typically total less each month than the total most households overspend on groceries. Consider opening a prepaid card just for groceries. There are a few cards out there with monthly fees of five dollars or less. Avoid any card with higher fees; they're not likely worth the extra charges. Find a card that has no reload fees or that will waive those fees with an automatic or direct deposit and that will *not* allow you to overdraft or spend more than the amount that is on the card. Otherwise, they will likely hit you with overdraft fees of twenty dollars or more. Find a card that simply denies purchases when there is not enough money in the account, and, additionally, will not charge a fee for such purchase denials. Check out online comparison sites like the one at Bankrate.com (under their Credit Card section) to find the right card for your household. Then, use your prepaid card just for groceries. Leave other methods of payment (checkbook, cash, debit card, etc.) at home so that you're not tempted to just use another debit card or a check if your grocery bill is higher than expected.

All of these options essentially prohibit you from spending more than the amount of money you have planned for groceries. Having such spending barriers is not a bad thing.

When it comes to gasoline, consider options similar to those for groceries, especially if you're having a difficult time staying within the gasoline budget. Most gasoline companies have gift card options with minimal or no activation or reload fees.

When it comes to gift giving, one of the easiest methods is simply to follow these steps:

1. Determine how much you can afford to spend on gifts for the entire year.

2. Make a list of family members, friends, coworkers, and others (children's teachers, daycare staff, etc.) to whom you regularly give gifts (regularly can mean frequently or annually).

3. Simply divide the amount from step one by twelve to determine the amount of money to automatically transfer from your main checking account to a dedicated "gift giving" savings account. This is not a special type of savings account. It's simply a savings account that you open at your bank or credit union for the specific purpose of saving money for gifts. However, if talking about Christmas or other annual giving holidays, ask the bank or credit union if they actually *do* have an account just for such purposes. They may pay a special

interest rate, but they will also likely charge a penalty fee or take back that interest if any money is withdrawn early from that account. In the case of Christmas savings accounts, early is often anytime before November each year.

Online savings accounts (accounts at online financial institutions that do not have a "brick and mortar" branch in town) can also help you save for Christmas. I would suggest, however, that if you open an online savings account, do *not* get an ATM or debit card along with it. That would make it too easy to access the money. You want an account that is inconvenient to access. Smartypig.com is another online option that also comes with a built-in anti-impulse device (though that's not why they have the policy). You cannot close a Smartypig.com savings goal and transfer the money back into a main account within a five-day period of depositing money into the Smartypig.com account. So, at certain times of the month, Smartypig.com users are forced to wait upwards of a week to get money out. That should be sufficiently long enough to cool spending jets or think of another way to deal with wants and needs.

Now that we've made it this far into the book, I know that some might be hollering, "Hey Genius, what about the cash method?" Well, funny you should ask. Using a cash-only method can be a great tool to stop overspending and keep us from going into excessive consumer debt. It does, however, have its own drawbacks, dangers, and disadvantages, which I'll address in the next section. So, please, stop hollering at the book. You're scaring the children.

TODAY'S MONEY

Taking the Excitement Out of Your Finances

I don't remember how I happened upon his site, since I'm not a "This Old House–Mr. Fixit" type, but I came across a chart several years ago at BobVila.com that listed life expectancies of various household appliances. This chart made it clear to me that we actually *can* prepare for what otherwise might seem like an unexpected expense.

Too often, we're caught unprepared when a fridge dies, the water heater goes out, or the car keels over. Consequently, far too many of us turn to a credit card, an appliance store line of credit, or, worse yet, a payday lender to come up with cash to buy a new (or new-to-us) fridge. Each of these borrowing options come with what many of us feel to be excessive interest charges.

Knowing the reasonable life expectancy for the following items, though not an exhaustive list, can help us all prepare for their eventual replacement by saving monthly amounts that total the item replacement cost on or before the expected date of replacement. The following are estimates, of course. Some items will last much longer than expected while others will last, seemingly, until the day after the warranty expires:

Consumer Item: Life Expectancy in Years

Refrigerator: 14–17
Washer/Dryer: 13–14
Electric Oven/Range: 17
Dishwasher: 10
Microwave: 11

Central A/C: 15
Gas Water Heater: 11-13
Furnace: 18
Vehicle: 12 (150,000 miles)
Digital Television: 10–15

Taking the Excitement Out of Your Finances Step-by-Step

Now, let's get boring. Follow these steps to create the most boring household personal finance system possible (and thus the most exciting in the long-run):

1. Contact your utilities companies to set up a monthly "level pay." Arrange for the utility companies to take your monthly payment directly from your checking account on the due date.

2. Set up regular, automatic transfers of your budgeted grocery money from your main bank account to a second checking account, a grocery store gift card, or a prepaid Visa or MasterCard. Take only this dedicated "grocery" card or checkbook to the grocery store (no extra cash or other cards) so that you don't (can't) overspend.

3. Arrange as many monthly bills as possible to be paid automatically from your bank account and, ideally, in the same amount each month. Such accounts might include any debts you're repaying, Internet and paid television services, donations, and so forth.

4. Set up monthly automated transfers from your main checking account to savings and investment accounts at the same financial institution. If you're tempted to transfer that money back into your checking account, then you should transfer it to accounts at a different financial institution (bank, credit union, brokerage house, etc.). Regardless, these accounts should help you prepare for emergencies, for replacing household consumer items (appliances, furniture, electronics), for gift giving (birthdays, holidays, etc.), and other predictable or expected expenses.

Dos and Don'ts

▲ Do take an inventory of your home's consumer items (consider using a camera as well) that will eventually need to be replaced.

▲ Do look through old checkbook registers for clues to household expenses you could save for regularly.

▲ Do set up a holiday gift giving account at your bank or credit union and regularly transfer funds into it.

▽ Don't get lost in tiny details (i.e., don't inventory single items valued under $500).

▽ Don't open savings accounts at a financial institution that makes it too easy to transfer money back to checking or that is too close to your work or home.

▽ Don't forget to balance your accounts regularly.

FACTOID

Commercially-available home refrigerators were produced in the United States as early as the mid-1910s, but by 1927, a GE "Monitor Top" fridge was selling for $525.[1] That's the equivalent to about $6,600 in today's dollars. Just six years later, Frigidaire introduced a model selling for $96 (or $1,620 in today's dollars). Thank heavens for production efficiency!

PART FOUR

$

EVERYDAY SPENDING

8

CREDIT OR DEBIT OR CASH? OH MY!

What's the best way of paying for things? Cash? Debit Cards? Checks? Prepaid cards? Money orders? Wire transfers? Credit Cards?

There are various payment methods, and each has its own advantages and drawbacks. Some tend to have more financial disadvantages than others.

I've heard from a lot of very dedicated people that they have the best system for managing their money. Some devotees of one popular financial guru will say that cash is the only way to go. Others swear by prepaid cards and gift cards. Still others stay loyal to money orders and wire transfers because it's all they know or they've been blocked out of mainstream banking options.

Is there one answer that works for everyone in every situation? Of course not, no more so than if we said there was one shampoo that works best for everyone. Different methods of payment are appropriate in different situations. Let's go through them one by one. By the end of this chapter, you should be in a better position to determine which method works best for your lifestyle and financial needs.

1.   *Cash*. Cash is king. It's true. Without cash (whether in our wallets, bank accounts, or tied up in CDs and money markets),

there is no true financial security. To some, cash might seem "old school," but for others, a cash-only system seems to hold the key that will magically transport them back to a time when debt didn't exist and credit didn't lead people into financial holes they couldn't dig themselves out of. Like any rose-tinted glasses peering into history, such optimism is a bit too, well, optimistic. Don't get me wrong. I truly believe that there is a definite place for cash in daily, weekly, and monthly money management systems. Studies are pretty clear that, contrary to the old notion of cash burning a hole in your pocket, using cash actually means that most of us spend less each month than if we're using plastic (whether credit cards or debit cards). How much less? Keep reading to find out.

Who is the cash-only system for, and what are its advantages and disadvantages? The cash system is likely the best option for anyone or any household constantly in credit card debt or living paycheck to paycheck, finally ready to make a financial change for the better. Not only do we spend less using cash, we actually can't overspend. If we go into a store with only cash in our wallets (no plastic and no checks), we cannot overspend, unless we open up a store card account on the spot, which we hereby solemnly swear not to do in such cases. We'll address that in the chapter on Credit.

The challenges of a cash-only system are numerous and not trivial. First of all, there's the biggest challenge of all. How do we go from living paycheck to paycheck, making only minimum payments on credit cards, and using credit cards to purchase day-to-day items, without starting to bounce checks and miss debt payments? The answer to this will occupy chapter 10.

The second challenge actually is a bit trivial. It's inconvenient. We need to go to the bank or credit union regularly and withdraw the right amounts of cash in the right denominations to take care of all our bills. The strictest of cash-only crazies would also pay their bills in cash at the place of business rather than sending it by mail.

The third challenge is not as trivial as some make it appear to be. Using cash means never using credit cards. I can be just fine with that, until someone asks me (and many have) how they can build their credit without using credit. This question usually comes in the context of someone wanting to qualify for a home loan. The reality is that if we want to build credit, we actually have to use it. For the foreseeable future, there's no way around that. I'll go into this in detail in the chapter on credit. Besides, there's more to credit than just purchasing a home. Our credit reputation can often influence our employment applications, our apartment rental applications, our vehicle and homeowner's insurance premiums, our ability to get student loans for our children, any elective surgeries we want that are not covered by insurance, and more. So, if we choose to go cash-only, which I'm certainly not against since I often use the method in my own home, just be aware that there are tangible downsides to it. Often, the advantages outweigh the disadvantages.

2. **Debit Card.** This payment option has its advantages but also some definite downsides. Most people would think that debit cards are the best option for households trying to live within a budget. After all, we can't overspend with a debit card because it can only draw against the funds that are already in our checking account, right? Yes and no. Yes, debit cards draw the payment directly (and pretty much immediately) from our checking account. Theoretically, when we've spent all of the money in our checking account, our debit card should stop working. However, many people have opted in to overdraft systems that approve the purchase and then either charge the customer a hefty overdraft fee (commonly twenty to thirty dollars) or their financial institution takes the overdrawn amount directly from the customer's savings accounts with the same institution.

Even if we haven't opted into these overdraft programs, we need to be aware of the findings of a study on human nature when it comes to purchasing with plastic. It doesn't matter if we're talking about debit cards, credit cards, gift cards, or store cards, if it's plastic, we tend to spend upwards of 50 percent more than we would using cash or a check.[1] The difference can be dramatic and can dramatically impact a business' bottom line. In 1980, L. L. Bean began accepting credit cards and observed that customers using credit cards had average purchases 30 percent more than others.[2] Not coincidentally, Visa found in a study over six years ago that people using credit cards (which studies show we equate psychologically with debit cards when it comes to purchase amounts) spent 30 percent more than those who used cash.[3] So, if we're using a debit card for all of our purchases because we think it helps us to "control" our spending, might I suggest we consider switching to the cash-only method? We could save 10–50 percent immediately on our discretionary spending. For the average household, that could easily be $400 or so!

Another downside to debit cards starts with the security benefits built into the cards. Yes, if we lose our debit card and report it stolen within two business days of learning of its loss or theft, we'll likely get all of our money back, minus up to about fifty dollars (thanks to the Electronic Fund Transfer Act signed by President Carter all the way back in 1978),[4] even if someone used it fraudulently to drain our accounts. However, unlike credit cards, where the thief was actually spending the credit card company's money and not our money, losing a debit card might mean that we're out of money and out of luck for however long it takes our bank or credit union to resolve the fraud case (possibly several weeks). This is why most financial experts would recommend that we carry and use credit cards in situations when we can least afford to be without money, such as when traveling away from home. Still, we use debit cards regularly in our household, particularly for groceries and around town expenses.

3. **Checks**. It won't be too far in the future when a teenager or a young adult will ask us what the expression, "The check's in the mail" means. After all, many being born right now will likely never write a check. If they receive a check for payment, they'll take it to their financial institution, but not to deposit it. They'll go and ask them what it is and if it has any historical value.

Okay, so I'm not too optimistic about the long-term survival of our dear friend, the paper check. But what about now? Does it still make sense to use checks? Of course. A study by Dilip Soman found that using either cash or a paper check, because the purchase requires us to count out or write down the amount we're spending, actually leads us to spend less than if we were to use plastic.[5] However, in our world of instant everything, where an extra twenty-five seconds at the checkout stand is an eternity, checks are not so convenient. Plus, mailing checks will require the additional purchase of a postage stamp (another future relic from our present).

Are there any other benefits of using checks besides spending a little less? Some might think they're easier to track than electronic purchases, but that's not necessarily true. Bank statements automatically show either the name or the address of the business where we used our debit card.

Still others think checks are safer than debit cards or online payments. Again, not true. Electronic payments online are much safer than placing a check in the mail. Checks can be stolen (from our mailbox or from the recipient's mailbox), acid washed, and rewritten payable to the thief in any amount they choose. Yes, our financial institution has some safeguards against such fraud, but that doesn't make such experiences pain-free.

Still not a believer? Let's look at the bottom of a check. What do all those numbers mean? They include our financial institution's routing number and our account number. It doesn't take a deep thinker to figure out what kind of financial damage could befall us if those two numbers fell into the wrong hands.

Additionally, checks are no longer even accepted by many businesses. Many restaurants and gas stations have a sign stating that checks are about as welcome as the bubonic plague.

Finally, most banks or credit unions do not give us free boxes of checks. We're required to buy them. However, if we're only using a couple of checks each month, it is worth asking our financial institution to provide us with some temporary checks. Many will give us three to ten such checks each month at no cost.

4. **Bill Pay**. With the advent and maturation of free bill pay services from our financial institutions, why would we ever write another check anyway? We can use our free bill pay to send money to our brother-in-law for the sushi party we had (I did). We can use it to pay for our child's lunch at school (rather than using their online service that probably charges us a service fee). We can even use our free bill pay to make donations to our church or to our favorite charity. If the organization accepts checks, they'll accept bill pay. Even if they don't accept checks, we might be able to set up a direct transfer from our account to the organization's account. They just need to provide us with their account number, which they should since it's already printed on any check they issue themselves.

5. **Prepaid Cards**. Prepaid cards, including the prominent Green Dot Visa and the Bluebird American Express cards, have been growing wildly popular. Former and even some current bank and credit union customers who have incurred hefty overdraft or bounced check fees, in addition to those enduring mounting monthly account maintenance costs, have been turning to prepaid cards in droves. Not all prepaid cards,

though, are created equal. Green Dot currently charges its customers a hefty $5.95 a month while Bluebird advertises no fees other than some for uncommon situations. There are several others out there, including the ReadyCard and Suze Orman's Approved card. All cards have some fees, but some cards are all about the fees. Beware of cards with high-profile endorsements, because they can come with monthly fees of fifteen dollars just to carry the card. Ouch!

Currently, none of these cards report our usage to the credit bureaus, although Suze Orman has been touting her efforts to achieve just such an arrangement. Whether it actually happens is something we won't know for a while. Since using a prepaid card is technically (or even theoretically) NOT a form of borrowing money or repaying debts, I'd be surprised if the consumer reporting agencies go for anything like this. There's a reason they're known as "credit" bureaus, since they track credit-related activities.

However, one of the benefits to using a prepaid card is that we can't overspend with them. Check that. I should say "most" of them. Some will actually charge a fee if we try to make a purchase for an amount greater than what is on the charge card. Obviously, we should avoid such cards.

Generally, though, I can see a place for cards like these in household finances, particularly for variable expenses like groceries, entertainment, dining out, or chocolate. What? Don't all households have a chocolate category in their budget? After loading the budgeted amount for the month onto the prepaid card, we can use it till it's gone, but then it's gone. We leave the other methods of payment home, and we can't overspend.

While not technically the same thing as a prepaid card, gifts cards can be used in a similar fashion. Just be sure to understand all of the fees (purchase, loading, reloading, etc.) the gift card might carry, and steer clear of those that would be more expensive than the pre-paid cards referred to above.

6. ***Money Orders***. When I start talking about money orders, it means we're getting into some of the more expensive options when paying for goods and services. To those who use money orders, a $.50 or a $1.50 fee may not seem like much, the same way spending four dollars each day for energy drinks might not seem like much to caffeine junkies. Over time, these fees build up. If we use just eight money orders per month to pay for utilities, rent, cell phone, a couple of debts, and a mail order transaction, we could easily spend $75 to over $120 each year just in fees.

Additionally, money orders are typically limited in size to $1,000 or less. However, they do make for a decent payment option if we want to ensure the payment is not slowed by check processing or to avoid carrying a lot of cash to make a major purchase (such as buying a used car or buying something off of Craigslist or eBay).

7. ***Wire Transfers***. Wire transfers are expensive, easily costing twenty-five to fifty dollars to send (let alone the fee to "receive" the transfer) each time. A better alternative would be a prepaid card, such as Suze Orman's Approved card, that currently comes with four cards for three dollars per month and carries no international exchange fee. An individual in country ABC can open a prepaid card such as this and send a second card to the family member, friend, or associate in country XYZ. The individual in country XYZ can then use the card anywhere MasterCard is accepted.

8. ***Credit Cards***. Credit cards are a double-edged sword when it comes to using them for making purchases. On the one hand, they are very secure and safe to use. There are protections for the purchaser against fraudulence and, in some cases, even poor consumer service (geographic limitations apply). Additionally, most credit cards do not charge any interest if the balance is paid in full by the due date.

On the down side, there is, of course, interest. Since I began teaching money management back in 2004, the average credit card interest rate on standard cards has generally varied between 13.5–16 percent. Additionally, as mentioned earlier, if it's made of plastic, we're likely to spend 10–50 percent more on everyday purchases with a credit card (or debit card) than with cash or a check. Furthermore, I'm not a fan of credit cards that charge annual fees, even if they are travel reward cards. Most households are better off saving that annual fee and saving the additional charges they're likely to incur through just having and using a credit card.

9. **_Electronic Funds Transfer (EFT)._** For our purposes, the final method of payment to discuss goes by several common and not-so-common names: online payment, EFT, Automated Clearing House (ACH), direct transfer, account-to-account transfer, interinstitutional transfer, and more. Basically, an EFT is how I refer to payments made over the Internet that go from the bank or credit union directly to a merchant. While this sounds like the same thing as a bill pay, an EFT transaction is initiated by the merchant, not by us or our financial institution. Usually, we set up the payment at the merchant's website by providing them with our checking account number and our financial institution's nine-digit routing number.

I'm actually a big fan of EFTs. They may seem very similar to online bill pay, but when it comes to online bill pay, we can't actually control when a payment will arrive at its final destination. If I use my credit union's bill pay system to cover a credit card payment or a utility bill, and if that payment arrives a day or two late, guess who's responsible for paying any related late fee? Yup, I am.

If, on the other hand, I set up an EFT with that credit card or utility company, they now are responsible for drawing my payment from my bank or credit union. If they draw it a day late, it's their own system's fault and not mine, so I'm not responsible for a late payment.

The main challenge with EFTs is to set them up and then remember them. Make sure to note the date any EFT is scheduled to process so that you have sufficient funds in your checking account to cover the charge. Also, if you ever close either the merchant account or your checking account, make sure to cancel the EFT with the merchant.

Wendy and I have most of our bills set up to pay each month through EFTs: mortgage, utilities, credit card (full balance), insurance, and so forth. Plus, they're generally FREE!

Now that we've discussed the most common methods for making payments, we are better prepared to decide upon the method that fits our own various situations best.

TODAY'S MONEY

Credit or Debit or Cash? Oh My!

A student in one of my classes reacted with dismay when I suggested that we pay our set bills (such as utilities, mortgage, cell phone, Internet provider, etc.) online. I described how setting up accounts with these companies allows them to deduct our monthly payments directly from our checking accounts. My student was impatient to point out that he had set up online payments and that he had subsequently had to pay a number of late fees because his payments didn't always arrive on time.

To me, the fact that he said the word, "arrive," meant that he and I were not talking about the same payment method. I am generally a big fan of having payments "taken" out of our checking accounts by the company we owe money to. Such a payment method is known as an ACH payment ("Automated Clearing House"). On the other hand, my student was talking about online bill pay through his bank or credit union.

Once we were on the same page, I agreed with him. Using bill pay can be a great option so long as we schedule the payments far enough in advance to ensure they arrive before their due date.

The main note of caution regarding ACH payments is to make sure we don't let our account balance get so low that an unexpected or, more likely, an unrecorded ACH will overdraft our account.

Step-by-Step Credit or Debit or Cash? Oh My!

Determine which payment methods to use for your various household expenses based upon the following:

Method of Payment	Possible Costs to Use	Great for...	Not-so-great for...
Cash	None	Any in-person purchases that involve decision making: -Stores -Groceries -Clothing -Restaurants	Large purchases Traveling Purchases where receipts are not available
Check	Cost of Checks Postage	Mailed payments Same in-person purchases as Cash When you want the check to serve as a receipt	When money's tight and you might incur overdraft charges
Automatic Clearing House (ACH)	None	Direct payments to monthly bills (utilities on "level pay," cell phone, loans, etc.)	Bills that vary from month to month
Debit Card	Usually just fees, if any, related to checking account	Monthly, automated bills, particularly utilities that are set on "Level Pay" (Internet, Sewer/Water/Trash, etc.)	Day-to-day purchases (see Cash: Great for... above) When money's tight and you might incur overdraft charges

Method of Payment	Possible Costs to Use	Great for…	Not-so-great for…
Money Order	25¢ to $5.00 or more	Mailed payment when we do not have a checking account	Any payment that could be made by cash, check, debit card, ACH, or online bill pay
Credit Card	Annual fee Interest	Traveling (but within a spending plan!) Receiving extra insurance coverage on large and/or long-distant purchases	Day-to-day purchases (see Cash: Great for… above) Anything that will be worn out, used up, consumed or broken down before we pay it off
3rd Party Online Bill Pay	From $0 to $10 a month	Bills or payments with no exact deadline One-time payments to individuals or organizations	Deadline-based bills such as rent/ mortgage, loans, and utilities
Wire Transfer	$5-$15 or more	Immediately getting emergency cash long distances	Regular money "relocations" to family or friends outside the country
Pre-paid Card ("stored value")	$3/month on up	Children's allowances Large monthly expenses we'd like to "fix" in order to minimize overspending	Any payment that could be made by cash, check, debit card, ACH or online bill pay

FOOD FOR THOUGHT

According to an April 4, 2013 report, Javelin Strategy & Research forecasts that mobile payments (using smartphones with the ability to swipe a debit or credit card) will increase 1100% over the next five years. While still a small portion of overall point of sales transactions, mobile payments will infiltrate nearly all aspects of our personal financial lives in the coming few years.

Dos and Don'ts

▲ Do understand that the method of payment matters in real dollars in our wallets.

▲ Do plan ahead for payments. The more "rushed" the payment, the more we typically pay in fees.

▲ Do accept that there is almost always a better and more affordable way to pay for things in our household budget. Stay alert!

▽ Don't use payment methods that charge unacceptable fees (basically, any fee seems unacceptable to me).

▽ Don't carry excessive amounts of cash in your wallet or purse.

▽ Don't ever, ever, EVER write your PIN on your debit or ATM card!

9

WHO KNEW STUFFING ENVELOPES WITH CASH COULD BE SO FUN?

"There's no school like old school." "Classics never go out of style."
"If it ain't broke, don't fix it."

Whatever the expression, the sentiment appropriately describes my feeling about using the cash-and-envelope system for managing our household expenses. This method is a virtually foolproof way of living within (or even better, below) our means, avoiding credit card debt, and kick-starting our savings goals.

Don't get me wrong. There are some serious long-term drawbacks and shortcomings to this approach for managing our cash flow, but I believe this is probably the best option out there for those of us who need a serious check to overspending and continually spiraling into debt. If you've struggled with any of the following financial setbacks within the past twelve months, please take that as a sign that you should switch, at least for now, to the cash-envelope system:

¢ Bounced a check or two . . . or eleven

¢ Carried a balance on at least one credit card from month-to-month and paying interest on the account

¢ Have no savings to speak of

¢   Wished to work overtime or get a second job to cover basic living expenses

¢   Spent money on trivial stuff before priorities are met

¢   Taken out a cash advance on a credit card

¢   Used a payday loan, title loan, rent-to-own, pawn loan, or tax refund anticipation loan

The power underlying the cash envelope system is twofold:

First, it's simple. Put a predetermined amount of cash into an envelope for each household expense and use that cash throughout the month (e.g., $500 in a "Groceries" envelope, $25 in an "Entertainment" envelope, a "Christmas Gifts" envelope, etc.).

Second, you can't overspend. Once the cash from the envelope is gone, it's gone.

Voilà! That's it!

Of course, there are a few other keys to making this work. First, commit to yourself and, if you're married, to your spouse, to stick to the system. You must also absolutely take your debit and credit cards out of your wallet and leave your checkbook at home.

I like the suggestion several of my students have shared about placing credit, debit, and ATM cards in a cup of water and then placing them in the freezer. That way, when we feel the impulse to purchase something that we haven't been planning for, we will need to spend ten to twenty minutes or more defrosting the card. That brief cooling-off period (actually, a warming-up period) could give the rational spender inside of us enough time to take back control of our finances and put a halt to the impulse purchase.

Keep in mind that as (or if) we choose to proceed with the envelope system, it does not need to be a permanent program. Once we regain control of spending and establish a habit of short term savings and planning, it will eventually make more sense to move from the envelope system to savings accounts. There's nothing stopping us from opening up multiple savings accounts, one for each monthly expense and short term savings goal that we had envelopes for.

If we begin to feel that our finances are starting to head back down the road to chaos (a.k.a. overspending, no savings, credit card balances, etc.), we can always move immediately back onto the envelope system. Like an old friend, it will be there to get us through tough times.

TODAY'S MONEY

Stuffing Envelopes

We can all relate to the following scenario that illustrates the very reason why the envelope system can be such a powerful tool in our lives to help us avoid overspending.

Most all of us have done (or still do) this. It's the end of the day. We've had a long and stressful time at work, at an appointment or at home, when we suddenly realize that we're out of bread and milk. Being the savvy consumers that we are, we realize that simply going out for dinner (and probably breakfast tomorrow) means that we'll spend many times the amount of money we would spend just for a gallon of milk and a couple loaves of bread.

Unfortunately, and although we intuitively know this to be a bad idea, we stop at the grocery store on our way home.

Rule #1 of Grocery Shopping: Never shop when hungry!

When we arrive, our stomach has begun to rumble, and we can't wait to get home for dinner. As we walk into the store, the overwhelming smell of freshly-baked French bread hits us like a steamroller. Right then and there, we're toast. All intentions of walking out the store with just $10 worth of bread and milk are out the window. We grab a bag of snacks "just to get us home." We grab some cheese to go with the loaf of French bread that we hadn't planned on purchasing. "I might as well get a few things for lunch and dinner tomorrow while I'm here." And with that financially fatal phrase, "I might as well," our budget is shot. Instead of spending $10, we find that we leave the store with three or four bags of groceries (much of it pre-packaged and overpriced) that cost us $50 or more.

How did this happen? We went shopping while hungry, AND worse, we carried a debit or credit card. If we had taken in only $10 in cash, no matter how hungry or hurried we were, we could not possibly have overspent.

Cash-only is the only way to go for true blue overspenders, and the envelope system is the simplest and best cash-only system (doesn't hurt that it's mostly free as well). Ditch the cards and even the checkbook while we stuff our envelopes with cash until our discipline is sufficient to control our spending.

Step-by-Step Stuffing Envelopes

Each household's envelope system may, and probably will, look different. We can choose to use actual postal envelopes or we can use plastic pouches or we can use separate boxes or piggy banks. Some will have plain, handwritten labels while others may be colorful and clever enough to display even for the in-laws. Regardless, below are a few steps every system needs. Remember that our envelope system should not include expenses that we can automate through the merchant or through our financial institution's bill pay service.

1. Identify and make a list of monthly household spending categories that cannot be set up on an automatic payment plan. (Groceries, entertainment, fun money, dining out, date night/entertainment, gasoline, gift giving, vacation, recreation, etc...)

2. Choose an envelope-like receptacle where we can store cash and coins for each spending category we've identified in Step

3. Determine how many bills in each denomination we'll need for each of the categories in Step 1 and for all categories put together. We'll want to know this for Step 4.

4. The day we get paid, withdrawal cash from our financial institution account in the amounts and denominations identified in step 3.

5. Use only the cash from your envelopes for household expenses. Take your debit and credit cards out of your wallet and purse so you're not tempted to use them. If necessary, shred them.

FOOD FOR THOUGHT

The "Denomination Effect" refers to a phenomenon of consumer behavior studied by Priya Rhagubir and Mary Jacoby Fellow that says, in essence, that the larger the denomination of bill we have to spend, the less likely we are to spend it on small purchases. Translation? Don't carry lots of $1 bills. We're hesitant to break a $50 bill, particularly for a small, unnecessary purchase.

Dos and Don'ts

▲ Do be specific with the envelope labels (i.e. "Trip to the Coast" rather than, "Vacation")

▲ Do keep your envelopes in a safe place (not the car or where children and/or guests in your home might find them)

▲ Do leave debit and credit cards and checkbooks at home when shopping with cash

▽ Don't carry a lot of small bills in your purse or wallet

▽ Don't use the envelope system as a replacement for short-term savings accounts or long-term investment accounts

▽ Don't give up. It might take three or four months to really get the envelope system working in your household

10

FROM CREDIT CARD DEBT TO CASH ONLY WITHOUT BOUNCING PAYMENTS

For most households that are struggling from paycheck to paycheck (and that accounts for roughly six out of ten households on every block in America), moving from complete credit card dependence to the cash-only envelope system sounds like a great idea. However, these same households also know that quitting their credit cards cold turkey would mean that their payments to credit card companies (and to other creditors and accounts) would turn to rubber and begin bouncing higher than the New York City skyline.

If we're making only minimum payments on our credit cards while using them to finance groceries, gasoline, utilities, insurance, gifts, and more, we're likely carrying a balance of thousands of dollars from month to month. The average credit card balance per household in this country, as of the writing of this book, is approximately $12,000. At an average credit card interest rate of 15 percent APR, that means that the average American Household is paying $150 every month just in credit card interest. If that doesn't seem too bad, consider that such a monthly interest payment equates to $1,800 every year. What does $1,800 mean to your household? How would you spend $1,800 if someone gave it to you? Ah, let me count the ways:

1. Provide the family with nearly twice the Christmas of the average American household.[1]

2. Invest it in a mutual fund that earns the average annual market return of 9 percent, and it's a great bet that it would grow to over $100,000 in about twenty years (having only contributed $36,000).

3. Get an incredibly high-performance big screen HD television for the entertainment room.

4. Pay for super premium cable or satellite television channel packages for a year.

5. Buy a 27-inch iMac or four iPad 2s.

6. Go on a week-long Caribbean or Hawaiian cruise.

We should never, ever say something like, "It's just $150. We can afford that." Instead, mentally equate the dollar amount with what it could be exchanged for that is something you really want to have or would like to do.

Now that you have a vision of what you're missing by paying so much credit card interest each month, how do you get rid of that interest without wreaking havoc on your bank account? The answer is: one step at a time.

Most simply can't quit cold turkey. Unfortunately, that's what many financial gurus, in their impractical brilliance, fail to mention when they glibly say, "Stop using your credit cards and go cash only."

No duh, but how?!

Once you understand what your income and expenses are each month and have put together a spending plan, you can start converting one or two monthly credit card purchases into cash transactions (by cash, I mean debit, bill pay, actual cash, check, or other direct debit method of payment). I suggest beginning with the non-set-in-stone expenses, such as gasoline, gifts, entertainment, or, if we're feeling particularly brave, groceries. First, determine how much you typically spend on the item or activity during the month, then take that amount out of your checking account right after payday (in cash, by writing the check, or by initiating an online bill payment).

That's it! For month number one, you've transferred one or two expenses from your credit card addiction to the cash-only envelope system.

During month number two, since your credit card bill will ask for a smaller minimum payment because you charged less during the previous month, you may now transfer another monthly purchase from the credit card to cash. Don't forget, though, to pay down the credit card balance by paying more than the minimum payment. Each month more purchases are transferred from a credit card to the envelope system, and within five or six months, most households will be weaned from using credit cards for regular purchases.

Besides this method, another option is to use unexpected or periodic "windfalls" to switch from the credit card habit to the envelope system. Probably the most common opportunity to do this occurs in mid to late spring when you receive a tax refund (*if* such a refund comes your way).

Let's say that you get a $1,000 refund this next year and are mentally and emotionally in a place to switch to the cash-only envelope system. If that's the case, take half of your refund and use it immediately to make some of the monthly purchases you habitually pay by credit card.

Going forward, you will continue to make those same purchases with cash, check, debit, or bill pay, never to return them to your credit card. That's $500 less each month that you'll be carrying on your credit card account, or approximately seventy-five dollars less each year in interest payments. Additionally, the monthly minimum payment will be about fifteen to twenty dollars less each month.

Now for the other half of your tax refund. Send that off immediately to your credit card company to bring the balance and, consequently, the minimum payment down. In fact, after using half of the tax refund for paying bills in cash and the other half for reducing credit card balance, your monthly minimum credit card payment will likely come down by approximately fifty dollars. As you continue to transfer one or two bills each month (insurance, Netflix, utilities, etc.) over to cash, pretty soon, you'll be paying all of your bills with cash, check, debit, or bill pay, and you can get rid of your credit card altogether.

Additionally, you should apply two powerful principles that help pay down and pay off credit card debt even *after* transferring all of your regular bills to cash. These principles are "level pay" and "PowerCash." Level pay is simply establishing the current monthly minimum payment as an ongoing monthly payment, even when the credit card company requests less. PowerCash, a term my financial educators and I created here at Debt Reduction Services, Inc. several years ago, refers to a relatively small but effective amount of money you "uncover" in your budget to help pay down debts or increase savings without the pain associated with across-the-board spending cuts in your regular spending.

TODAY'S MONEY

From Credit Card Debt to Cash Only WITHOUT Bouncing Payments

The highest credit card interest rate that I have ever heard of (and I'd be surprised if there aren't others even higher) was offered back in 2010 by a South Dakota credit card company. These cards, targeting sub-prime borrowers, came with credit limits of just $300 but smacked the card holders with a frightening 79.9% APR! On a maxed out card balance and making minimum payments, the annual interest paid would be somewhere in the stratospheric region of $200 to $225 (or 67% to 73% of the original balance). I wouldn't be surprised if the same company might be selling oceanfront property in the same part of that landlocked state?

Step-by-Step from Card to Cash

To go from credit card dependent to credit card free, follow the steps below in addition to the suggestions within the chapter:

1. From your previous credit card statements, figure out how much money you paid to your credit card companies over the past twelve months.

2. Write down one to three activities you would like to do or items you would like to purchase in the next twelve months and their rough cost (each should equal more or less the amount of Step 1).

3. Commit to self and spouse or best friend to get to a point over the next twelve months where you can begin to save the money from Step 1 rather than sending it to your credit card companies.

FACT

There are really only three factors in paying down our debts, and they all involve getting more money to go toward our debt's principle balance rather than to its interest:

1. Earn more to send a larger payment;
2. Spend less to send a larger payment;
3. Get a lower interest rate to increase the portion of our payment going to principle.

Typically, only factor #2 involves the self-discipline required for successfully paying down debts. Whether alone or in conjunction with #1 and/or #3, factor #2 almost always needs to be involved in paying off our debts.

Dos and Don'ts

▲ Do identify each week or month which purchase or purchases to switch from credit card to cash.

▲ Do commit to quitting by telling family members and close friends.

▲ Do look ahead to potential income windfalls (e.g. tax refunds) and plan to send it off (or a large portion of it) as a credit card payment.

▽ Don't quit credit cards cold turkey without a plan.

▽ Don't simply transfer debt from one card to another (regardless of differences in interest rates) without establishing barriers to our spending.

▽ Don't apply for ANY new credit cards, retail cards, gas cards, or other debts while paying down our current debts.

PART FIVE

$

EVERYDAY CREDIT (RE)BUILDING

11

PLEASE TELL ME WHAT MY CREDIT SCORE REALLY MEANS!

What is a good credit score?

A lot of confusion exists when it comes to credit scores and credit reports. To begin with, many of us speak of credit, credit scores, credit reports, credit risk, credit files, credit ratings, credit histories, credit worthiness, credit checks, credit backgrounds, and credit records without really knowing the difference or if there even is a difference.

First of all, there is no practical difference between the terms credit history, credit record, credit file, and credit report. They all refer to a collection of our past credit-related activities (loans we've taken out, collection accounts we have, credit cards we've opened or closed, etc.) from the past seven to ten years, whether or not those accounts are open or closed. Personally, I use the term Credit Report, but feel free to use any of the terms.

While there is no practical difference between the terms credit score, credit rating, credit risk, and credit worthiness, they do differ from a credit report. I typically use the term Credit Score. A credit score is like a school grade. It's a credit scoring model (and there are over a thousand of them nationwide) that processes much of the information on our credit reports, regarding some data as more important than others, to estimate how much of a risk we currently are and will be in the near future to potential lenders. The higher the score, the less of a risk we theoretically pose for defaulting on (not paying back) our loans in the future.

If we have less-than-stellar credit, the reason or reasons for our poor rating do not matter. Some of us might think this unfair, especially when we have been dealing with massive medical-related debts that are beyond our control. We ask, "Why should we be punished with poor credit for something that is not our fault?"

Having such a point of view indicates that we think credit is a reflection of our efforts and our character rather than, again, what it truly represents: the risk we represent of defaulting on current and future debts. No matter the reason, whether we're experiencing financial hard times due to medical debts, job loss, or poor money management, the reality is that given these situations, we're at a much higher risk for not being able to pay our debts on time, going forward.

Take the lenders' point of view for a moment. They have to consider how much risk they're willing to take with the money we're asking to borrow. Let's be honest, whether we currently have or recently had trouble making medical bill payments or struggle with paying our department store card on time, the reality is that we have trouble paying our debts. The reason is irrelevant to potential lenders. If they didn't care, they'd be a charity rather than a business.

So, how should excellent credit be defined if not by effort? The most common practice among lenders is to use a rating system, and the most common credit rating service is FICO (the common acronym for the company that pioneers credit ratings: Fair Isaac Company). Our FICO score can range from 300 on the low end to 850 at the top. So, while many lenders and even credit experts (including me) will refer to an excellent credit score being in the 750 to 760 range on up, the reality is that we cannot actually define what an excellent credit score is.

Remember, the score defines or delineates risk, and since each individual creditor has their own risk tolerance, each of them gets to determine what credit score (risk level) they consider to be excellent. In essence, when a lender offers their best repayment terms (interest rates, promotional offers, etc.), they consider the borrower to have excellent credit.

Consequently, we can't expect all creditors to offer their best repayment terms to the exact same pool of borrowers. The lender that can absorb financial loss better might be willing to take greater risks than a smaller company that's more vulnerable to such occurrences. Hence, the company that is able to risk more can afford to offer better rates to borrowers with lower scores (and higher potential for defaulting). That doesn't mean the more vulnerable company won't risk as well. They will sometimes offer loans to riskier borrowers, but risk is conversely tied to reward, so we should expect such loans to carry higher interest rates. This is the lender's reward for taking a great chance on those with lower credit scores.

To summarize, then, credit scores do *not* indicate how much money we can borrow. They do *not* indicate whether we are a good person or a bad person. They may or may NOT indicate whether we are trying to be financially responsible, since the reasons for our poor credit may be out of our control. Credit *does* attempt to project at what level of risk we (or individuals like us who have similar credit backgrounds and activities) are for missing payments and defaulting on loans currently or in the near future.

Looking at our credit rating this way, what else do we learn? First, we understand why certain items are tracked while others aren't. Unless it's statistically possible to connect the item or the activity to higher default rates, it's not a valid indicator of our credit rating.

We also learn why most of our credit-related activities no longer impact our rating after seven years. The further in the past our payments, overdue bills, and collection accounts are, the less likely they are to be reliably indicative of our future behavior.

Some have probably heard that the best indicator of future behavior is past behavior. I think we'd all agree that it would be acceptable to amend this to read, "The best indicator of near future behavior is recent past behavior." Many of the choices and behaviors I exhibited ten, fifteen, or twenty years ago no longer have any similarity, thank heavens, to the way I act and behave today. However, the choices I've made in the past year or two are much more likely to be similar to the choices I will continue to make in the next couple of years.

The best indicator of near future behavior is recent past behavior.

I like that as a definition of credit. I'll think I'll stick with it.

TODAY'S MONEY

Credit Score

I'll admit that I laugh pretty hard at the commercials for some of the credit scores available for "free." One even has the YouTube community try to outbest (successfully in my opinion) their own advertising department. The problem with these "free" credit scores is twofold. First, most are designed to be anything but free, and second, they attempt to walk the line that would mislead us into thinking that their credit scores are the ones that really matter, when they really don't.

Most free credit scores are only provided AFTER you sign up for a trial period of some credit monitoring service that can cost anywhere from $17 to $20 per month (that's $204 to $240 per year)!

Here are a couple of the disclosures you'll find that come with these offers:

"This score is intended for your own educational use. There are numerous credit scores and models available in the marketplace and lenders are likely to use a different score when evaluating your creditworthiness." (Equifax)

"Calculated on the PLUS Score model, your Experian Credit Score indicates your relative credit risk level for educational purposes and is not the score used by lenders."

That's their way of saying that no lenders actually use these particular scores when determining your creditworthiness. Still, I do believe that patterns in these free scores can help us become aware of unexpected changes on our credit reports.

I just strongly urge against paying for their monthly monitoring services.

The only score that really matters when it comes to qualifying for a loan is the FICO score, which you may purchase at www.myfico.com (currently for $20 each).

Step-by-Step Credit Score

Here are three services that I'm aware of (and actually use) to access some of these free credit scores. They limit how often you may check your score, and they are, as noted above, for educational purposes only. Still, I watch them for changes in my scores that might indicate problematic (i.e. unauthorized) activity on my credit reports.

I need to give a standard disclaimer here, indicating that the listing of these services below does not constitute an endorsement or a guarantee of them in any way, shape, or form. You need to do your own research prior to signing up for these services.

1. My current favorite is CreditKarma.com. Each month I get a free and fairly up-to-date TransRisk score (based on TransUnion credit report) along with information about how my score might also impact the interest and even the car insurance premium I pay. I would just suggest that you DON'T sign up for their email list service.

2. CreditSesame.com is another site that I've recently begun using. It will even notify me when something changes on my Experience credit report. So far, I'm impressed and pleased with this site, and I get an updated Experian-based score each month.

3. Quizzle, another truly free credit score site, can provide you with a score based upon your Experian credit report. However, you can only get an updated Quizzle score every six months.

FOOD FOR THOUGHT

Although very simplified, the information below describes the five major factors contributing to our FICO credit score, along with their relative importance. Author of *The Road to 850*, Al Bingham actually identifies more than 40 credit score factors in great detail, but they breakdown into the following:

1. Payment History: 35% (At least the minimum payment is on time every month)

2. Amounts Owed: 30% (The lower the balances on our accounts the better)

3. Length of Credit History: 15% (The older our accounts the better)

4. New Credit: 10% (The fewer loan and credit card applications the better)

5. Types of Credit Used: 10% (The more varied our credit "portfolio" the better, although I would never advise you to open different accounts just to improve this portion)

Do's and Don'ts

▲ Do get your FICO scores, even though you have to buy them, a year or two ahead of purchasing or refinancing a home

▲ Do focus on paying your debts as agreed in order to build your credit scores

▲ Do consider dramatic changes in your credit score as potential signs of identity theft

▽ Don't sign up for trial services just to get a "free" credit score

▽ Don't be surprised if one of your "FAKO" credit scores is different from your FICO by 75 points or more

▽ Don't believe the myth that checking your own credit will hurt your credit score. It does not

12

BUILDING CREDIT ONE STEP AT A TIME

When building credit from scratch (as most young adults must) or rebuilding credit after a run of difficult financial challenges (medical collections, bankruptcy, job loss, etc.), there are several steps to take to improve credit scores and show potential creditors that we are not a high credit risk to them (so that they'll charge a lower interest rate).

Correct and Confirm

First of all, you want to ensure that your credit history is accurate and "clean." Clean does not mean perfect. It just means that the information listed on the report is accurate. To get a truly free copy of your credit report, start at www.AnnualCreditReport.com. This site does NOT require a credit card or debit card number or to sign up for any trial offers for a ten- to twenty-dollar-per-month service that you don't need (and probably do not even want). This is a federally mandated website where everyone can get a free, no-strings-attached credit report from each of the three major credit bureaus every twelve months. And to bust a popular myth, checking your credit does not hurt your credit rating or affect your ability to qualify for a loan.

While not a must, you may also consider monitoring your credit more frequently than this service provides. There are a couple of ways to do this: (1) sign up for fifteen-dollar-per-month credit monitoring service, or (2) sign up for a free monthly credit score at a site such as CreditKarma.com to watch for concerning trends on a regular basis.

You may also call to request a free credit report toll-free at (877) 322-8228 or by mailing a request to Annual Credit Report Request Service, PO Box 105281, Atlanta, GA, 30348-5281.

Note that you should ideally use the form provided through the FTC at

www.consumer.ftc.gov/articles/pdf-0093-annual-report-request-form.pdf.

Once you have your credit report in hand (or have access to viewing it online), make sure you recognize the information it contains. Are the names listed on the report yours? Do you recognize the street addresses? Do you recognize the creditors and accounts, including collection agencies, credit card companies, home and auto lenders, and others? If any of this information is inaccurate, or if the accounts are not even yours (which, according to a 2013 FTC report is the case in about one-in-four consumer's reports), you can dispute them pretty easily online. While there is no guarantee the information will be corrected quickly, it's definitely what you want to do.

Utilities/Cell Phone

Once you've disputed inaccurate information on your report, the next few steps to (re)building your credit are small ones, but at least they are free. If you have a history of on-time payments to your utilities or cell phone company (not including a prepaid phone service), write them a cordial letter or call them, using your nicest voice, to request that they report your payment history to the credit bureaus.

They are not required to do this and typically do not do so auto-matically. However, if they do, it can have a good, albeit rather small, impact on your credit.

Authorized User

Next, especially if you're young or new to credit, consider asking a close family member with good credit (most often a parent) if they would be willing to add you to their credit card account as an au-thorized user. This is not the same thing as being a cosigner or joint owner of the account. Authorized users are not ultimately respon-sible for paying the account, but they are issued a card with their name on it that looks and acts like any other credit card. In some cases, if you have to gently persuade family members, you could explain that they don't need to give you the card at all. They can request that it be sent to their address, and they can even shred it upon receipt. By the mere fact that you are an authorized user on an account in good standing, you inherit some of the account holder's good credit vibes.

Be aware, though, that there was enough abuse of this in the mid 2000s that FICO eliminated this practice as a credit score factor for a while, until public uproar forced their hand into bringing it back. Unfortunately, there had been quite a few "entrepreneurial" spirits out there who were selling their good credit to those in need and requesting authorized user cards in the buyers' names. Essentially, this became a method of "playing the system" to inaccurately build a credit rating that was better than it should have reflected. Although it was brought back, the impact on the score of being an authorized user is not quite as positive as it used to be.

The remaining steps in building or rebuilding credit involve actually applying for and using lines of credit. The inclination of many of us is to go right for the big ones, applying for a Visa, MasterCard, American Express, or Discover Card from a national bank. Unfortunately, most of these applications will be denied, due to insufficient credit history. This leads to the common and understandable question, "How am I supposed to build my credit history if I can't get credit to begin with?" It appears to be a case of the chicken and the egg.

When building (or rebuilding for that matter) your credit, remember to start small and start local.

To apply a mixed metaphor, "Which came first? The chicken or the egg?" Answer: the wheel.

Tire Store

Yes, the lowly tire is a great place to start building credit.

If you own a vehicle and it needs tires anyway, I suggest that you put aside enough money in a savings account until you can afford to purchase the tires in cash. However, instead of paying at the register with cash or a check, apply for a line of credit from the tire store. Many tire stores use in-house financing and are typically more liberal in their approval process. More often than not, though, the interest rates on these lines of credit seem astronomical, often in the mid to upper 20 percent range.

After getting approval, I suggest paying the account off quickly, say, in just one or two months. This will minimize the amount of interest you pay (and I'm certainly no fan of paying interest) while also building your credit.

Remember, though, throughout this whole process of building credit, to ask why you even want to build your credit in the first place. It should NEVER be simply for the sake of building your credit.

Credit is meant to help you make major purchases in your life. There can be expenses associated with building and then using credit, so even though there are numerous people and organizations looking at your credit outside of lending, it's better to have no credit than bad credit.

Also, keep in mind that as I make suggestions about applying for lines of credit to build or rebuild credit history, you should never apply for more than one or two lines of credit per year. That includes store cards, credit cards, bank loans, car loans, home loans, and so forth.

Retail or Gas Card

That said, six to twelve months later, consider applying for a store or gas card. Again, such creditors tend to be more generous with their approvals. Easy credit, though, also tends to mean expensive credit. Most store cards and gas cards have interest rates in the upper teens to upper 20 percent range. Ouch!

I'll use an example from my own experience. Back when my first-born was about three or four years old, I planned to take him on a six-hour road trip to visit family. That much time in the car with a toddler required a plan of action or it would lead to certain insanity. So, I did some searching and some comparison price shopping and found a TV/VCR combo (remember those dinosaurs?) at a local Target store for $200.

I arrived at the store fully intending to make the purchase with a check (another dinosaur). However, the cashier asked if I'd like to save an additional 15 percent, I believe, on my purchase by applying for and putting the purchase on a Target card. It had been some time since I had opened a new line of credit, so I took a few moments (probably too many for those in line behind me) to calculate my savings if I were to accept the offer. That was a thirty-dollar savings, and I was at the time a single, self-employed dad to whom thirty dollars was (and still is) a fair amount of money.

A minute or two later, the cashier handed me a small piece of white paper, indicating that it was my temporary card with my new account number on it. Target hoped (as any retailer would) that I would then leave the store with my purchase and with a balance owed to them and promptly forget about paying it off until I got my bill. Most people do this, and when they receive the bill thirty days or so later, find that they've spent most of the money intended for the original purpose and are now "trapped" in the cycle of making only minimum payments. Again, OUCH!

I can't take credit for making my next move through any intelligent design on my part. I simply followed an impression and walked straight from the cashier, fifteen feet across the aisle to the customer service desk, handed them my temporary card and told them I would be paying off the balance of my account with a check. So, I walked in intending to pay $200 plus sales tax, and I walked out having paid only $170 plus sales tax. Additionally, I now had a new account on my credit history that, for the next ten years, was listed as open and "paid as agreed."

The danger of such a strategy involves what one of my students recently shared that regularly happens to her friend. Whenever she is offered a discount for applying for a store card, she takes it. Her credit is terrible, but she wants that discount. She gets the discounts, so one might be wondering, "Why not? She's taking advantage of the stores. What's the problem?"

The problem is that she, like a third of the population with credit or retail cards in their purses or wallets, ended up making ONLY the minimum payments on those accounts. That leads to a seemingly endless cycle of repayment, since only about 1 percent of most minimum payments actually go toward lowering the principle or balance on the account. The rest goes toward interest—or profit—in the stores' pockets. That's why stores can afford to offer such discounts to their customers. In fact, nowadays, many retailers—and I'm thinking of electronics and furniture stores—earn about half of their annual revenue not from what they actually sell, but from finance charges to their customers. Again, that's why so many will offer seemingly great terms such as "same as cash" for three, six, or twelve months or more. They know that a very large percentage of customers who take advantage of these offers will eventually carry a balance beyond the original term, which, if we read the fine print, not only nullifies the "same as cash, no interest" offer going forward but actually means that the store goes back and tacks on interest to the balance of the loan every month from the beginning of the account as if the "same as cash" offer never existed. Double OUCH!

As Exhibit A, having learned the ups and downs of credit through my own mistakes allows me to share an experience with my second line of credit, recalling that my first credit experience was to max out a $2,000 Discover Card at 19.99% APR in just thirty-six hours. When I was twenty-three years old, I applied for and was approved for a $500 Chevron card. I was at college and happened to live across the street that year from a Chevron station. Not surprisingly, I ended up using that card for much more than gas. I purchased bread, candy bars, soft drinks, chips, and other college staples at the card's 25% APR and had that card maxed out before the end of its first semester in my wallet. In fact, by Christmas break, due to late fees and over-the-limit fees, my balance exceeded $800. Even my own teenaged children would probably respond, "Duh, Dad! What were you thinking?!"

I wasn't. I was part of the financially undead, wandering from offer to offer seeking to finance my lust to consume. Unfortunately, many of us tend not to use much logic when it comes to using credit.

Rather, we react to impulse, and my impulse always seems to carry me towards chocolate and sweets.

In the end, I ended up settling with Chevron to pay it off for less than what was owed, meaning that my credit really suffered for a while.

Secured Card

A secured credit card can be a great credit building product, but it can also be a drain on your wallet. Many, though not all, financial institutions offer them.

Typically, the process involves opening up and depositing a significant amount of cash (usually $300 to $1,000 or so) into a secured savings account at the financial institution. They then issue a credit card (looks and is accepted as payment just like any major credit card) with a limit equal or close to the amount you have deposited into the secured account. By secured, though, you need to understand that you cannot touch the money in the saving account as long as the credit card is open and active. If you miss a payment or incur a penalty fee, it will likely come from your secured savings account, and the card might be deactivated until you pay the fees and return the secured account to the original balance.

Secured cards, as I mentioned, act just like any other Visa or MasterCard credit card and can help to build a history of on-time credit card payments. I have two major concerns, though, with secured cards.

First, they always carry fees of some sort. Whether we're talking about a high annual fee, monthly fees or, in some cases I've seen "per transaction" fees, be aware that these "products" are typically much more expensive than standard credit cards. This is why I typically do not suggest to my classes that people use them UNLESS they're dead-set on buying a home within the next couple of years and really need to build or rebuild their credit rating.

Second, though, is the real kicker. I've talked to a number of students in my classes who tell me that after using a secured card for a year or more, paying the additional fees, and ensuring their payments were made on time, they applied for a regular credit card only to find out that their secured card usage was not even being reported to the credit bureaus. Consequently, they never received credit for their history of on-time payments.

I suggest, then, that if you're certain you want to go with a secured credit card, make sure to get in writing that the financial institution will actually report your payments and credit activity to at least one, if not all three, of the major consumer reporting agencies.

Credit Builder Loans

Over the past few years, I've heard more and more publicity, advertisements, and word-of-mouth chatter about so-called "credit builder" loans. They are offered by banks and credit unions and appear to be a potentially beneficial product for building credit. They do, as with most of these options, come with their own costs and drawbacks. Here's how they typically work:

If you've filed for bankruptcy or for other reasons have a poor credit rating, you can apply for a credit builder loan of around $500 or $1,000. Let's use the $1,000 loan example. Say that you apply for a $1,000 credit builder loan and the bank approves you at a fairly reasonable rate (usually in the upper single-digit APR range). They set up a monthly repayment plan, and for the next year, you make those monthly payments to the bank. All the while, the bank is reporting your monthly payments to one or more of the credit bureaus. However, have you noticed anything missing so far? Yes, the money!

You don't actually get the money until you've "repaid" the loan. In the meantime, they actually do deposit that $1,000 into an account, much like the secured savings account related to the secured credit cards. You will probably even earn an infinitesimal amount of interest on that $1,000 over the course of the loan. However, this is a loan only in the very loosest of terminology. In practice, it's a forced savings account with a negative interest rate. Still, I applaud those banks and credit unions who are offering these types of products so that individuals can begin to prove (or in some cases, disprove) that they are ready for the next step—the "Big One" —in building their credit.

Major Credit Cards

When it comes to building or rebuilding a credit rating, no account, no line of credit, no product is as influential as the major credit card. Even mortgages, car loans, and students loans, although typically much larger than the credit card limit, don't have as great an impact on credit rating as the major credit card does. Why is that so? Because managing a credit card takes greater self-control and financial "maturity." Taking care of a monthly installment loan is easy. Make the same payment every month, and you typically can't add any additional balance to the account. A credit card, on the other hand, requires self-restraint and a determination to pay it off or at least pay it down each month.

For this purpose, getting approved for a major credit card is often more difficult than getting approved for most other forms of credit (excepting a mortgage). Once you've spent a year or two responsibly using and building your credit following some of the steps mentioned previously, you may be ready to apply for a major credit card. I generally suggest to first approach your own credit union or bank to ask for a low-limit card of $300 or $500. Of course, if you don't have a checking account or have not had, shall we say, a positive experience with one, you may need to look elsewhere.

Oddly enough, and although likely disputed by credit union fans, credit cards issued by credit unions do not have as great an impact on our credit score as do those issued by national banks,[1] which is why we will eventually want to apply for a credit card from one of the larger national banks.

Regardless of the type of credit, make sure to make at the very least the minimum payment every month, on time. Ideally, you should make the full balance payment. It is a myth that in order to build an excellent credit rating, you must carry a balance on your credit cards. Those who make such suggestions, and Al Bingham would probably agree that far too many of them are mortgage brokers, are doing a disservice to their clients.

Make only purchases you would make anyway with cash and pay the balance off by or before the due date. Voilà, credit built! Now wasn't that simple?

TODAY'S MONEY

Building Credit

Back when my first born child was about three or four years old, I was planning to take him on a six hour road trip to visit family. That much time in the car with a toddler required a plan of action, or it would lead to certain insanity. So, I did some price comparison shopping and found a TV/VCR combo (remember those electronic dinosaurs?) at a local Target store for $200.

I arrived at the store fully intending to make the purchase with a check (another dinosaur). However, the cashier asked if I'd like to save an additional 15%, I believe, on my purchase by applying for and putting the purchase on a Target card. It had been some time since I had opened a new line of credit, so I took a few moments (too many probably for those in line behind me) to calculate my savings if I were to accept the offer. That was a $30 savings, and I was at the time a single, self-employed Dad to whom $30 was (and still is) a fair amount of money.

A minute or two later, the cashier handed me a small piece of white paper, indicating that it was my temporary card with my new account number on it. I'm sure that Target hoped (as any retailer would) that I would then leave the store with my purchase with a balance on my account and promptly forget about paying it off until I got my bill. Most people do so, and when they receive the bill 30 days or so later, they find that they've spent most of the money intended for the original purpose and are now "trapped" in the cycle of making only minimum payments. Again, OUCH!

I can't take credit for making my next move through any intelligent design on my part. I simply followed an impression and

118

> walked straight from the cashier, fifteen feet across the aisle to the customer service desk, handed them my temporary card and told them I would be paying off the balance of my account with a check. So, while I walked in intending to pay $200 plus sales tax, I walked out having paid only $170 plus sales tax. Additionally, for the next ten years, I had an account with a $0 balance on my credit history that was listed as open and "paid as agreed."

Step-by-Step Credit Score

Here are seven steps to building (or rebuilding) your credit history over the next 24 months or so, remembering that no amount of "tricks" and no credit report company can rebuild credit if you're in the habit of missing payments and maxing out cards. On time payments and paying down your debts can account for 65% of your credit score.

1. Month 1: Ask your utilities and cell phone companies to report your history of on time payments to the credit bureaus. NOTE: They do not do so automatically, so ask nicely, and allow at least one month for this information to be listed on your credit reports.

2. Month 2: Consider asking a family member (parent) with good credit to ask their card company to issue you an authorized user card on their account. NOTE: This option is particularly meant to help the teens and young adults in our lives but it can be helpful for adults as well. Allow at least one month for such an account to begin impacting your credit.

3. Months 2-12: Apply for no more than one or two new accounts a year, starting with a tire store line of credit, followed by a retail (store) account and/or a gas station card.

4. Months 12-18: Look into credit builder loans at a bank or credit union. Essentially, these are forced savings accounts with negative return that report our monthly "deposits" as credit payments.

5. Month 18-24 (if Step 4 is NOT unsuccessful): Ask bank or credit union for a low credit limit credit card.

6. Month 18+ (if Step 5 is NOT successful) Shop around for a secured credit card. NOTE: These can carry high annual, if not monthly, card fees.

7. Month 24+: Apply for a Visa or MasterCard from a major national bank.

FACTOID

According to FICO (as quoted by Bankrate.com), the median credit score in the US is 723. That jives with estimates I've seen between 720 and 725.

Do's and Don'ts

▲ Do make at least the minimum payment due on any debt payments.

▲ Do whatever is possible to keep accounts from going to collections. NOTE: work out payment arrangements with your original creditor AS SOON AS a collections notice is received.

▲ Do pay down debt balances.

▽ Don't carry a balance just to build credit. Our score can be positively affected even if we pay of our balance every month in full.

▽ Don't close old credit accounts that are in good standing (unless they're charging fees).

▽ Don't fall for the minimum payment trap. Making only minimum payments on credit card accounts leads to 15 to 25 years of debt.

13

CHECK YOUR CREDIT WITHOUT HARMING YOUR CREDIT (OR YOUR WALLET)

One of the questions on the survey we give to those filing for bankruptcy and taking our debtor education course asks them where they can go to get a free (truly free), no-strings-attached and no-credit-card-required credit report. The majority respond that FreeCreditReport.com is the correct answer. Unfortunately, the respondents are great examples of how effectively a catchy name and good marketing campaign can influence us. FreeCreditReport.com, a subsidiary of the consumer reporting bureau, Experian, offers a free credit report, but with a catch: you must sign up for a trial to their credit monitoring service. If you do not cancel within their trial period (currently just seven days from the sign-up day), they begin charging your debit card or credit card, which was provided to them during the trial registration process, a monthly "membership" fee of $19.99.

I'm not disputing or discussing the value of FreeCreditReport.com's credit monitoring service or similar services of other credit monitoring businesses. They provide something that many consumers obviously want: notification if something goes wrong on their credit reports.

However, we need to remember that the only federally mandated website where we can get a free credit report from each of the three main credit bureaus is AnnualCreditReport.com. When this site went into effect at the end of 2004, nobody in my classes had even heard that there was a possibility of getting a truly free credit report.

However, I have seen a gradual growing awareness among consumers around the country when it comes to this program. It is refreshing to hear one or two individuals in each credit class speak up and encourage others to use AnnualCreditReport.com rather than these bait-and-switch types of programs.

Then there are those who insist on continuing to use these monthly subscription services because they believe this is the only way for them to get a "free" credit score. To those individuals, I would say, yes, you're getting a free score, but what does that score mean, who uses it, and for what purposes? The sad reality is that such scores only provide us with indications and patterns in our credit worthiness. Typically, though, no lenders actually use these credit scores as the basis for the approval or denial of a loan application. There really is only one credit score that matters in this country, and that is the FICO score.

FICO is the name of the company that pioneered the credit scoring model. Originally Fair, Isaac, and Associates, then the Fair Isaac Corporation (2003), the organization went through another official name change recently in 2009 and is now just FICO.[1]

In essence, FICO takes data contained in each of the three credit reports (assembled by the three nationwide consumer reporting agencies: Equifax, Experian, and TransUnion), weighs some of the data more heavily than others, and produces a score between 300 and 850. The higher the score, the lower the potential risk we are to lenders of defaulting (not paying) on loans. In other words, the higher the score, the better. These scores are made available to lenders during the loan application process.

Each of the three consumer reporting agencies sells a "credit score" that they say is similar to the score used by creditors. However, the reality is the scores that can be purchased or received through such free trial offers are only "FAKOS" (fake FICOS) and FICO wannabes.

To get your real FICO scores, you have to go to myfico.com and pay about twenty dollars for each credit bureau score.

Does that mean that the other credit scores being sold or given to consumers are useless? I believe they can still serve a purpose. As long as we're not using them as a basis for making borrowing decisions, they can help us to understand patterns in our credit. As an example, I use the free TransUnion score available through CreditKarma.com. Each month, they allow me to access my TransRisk score for free. If I were to notice my credit score taking a dip, that would give me cause for concern, and I would look into the matter more closely to see why. Significant drops in the score would indicate that there are some unauthorized activities happening on my credit.

Otherwise, I typically get my credit report from AnnualCreditReport.com every four months. While it's not a perfect system, it can help to minimize the results of identity theft on my credit.

Consumer credit protection and identify theft recovery experts would be quick to say, though, that checking your credit once every four months is likely not enough. If someone steals your identity and uses it for four months before you learn about the theft, there's likely to be a massive amount of damage to deal with. As mentioned before, there are several credit monitoring services available for a fee, and some also come with a type of credit repair insurance. Don't pay more than ten to fifteen dollars a month for individual coverage from such services, and don't let anyone scare you into signing up for expensive services you're unsure about. The financially devastating forms of identity theft, while growing in the United States, are still fairly uncommon.

Sixty-four percent of the nearly nine million American households that are victims of identity fraud each year experience such theft in the form of unauthorized or fraudulent credit card charges.[2] The vast majority of expenses resulting from such cases are absorbed by the credit card companies directly (and indirectly by card holders and merchants) and not by the victims. If you're careful with your credit and keep your identifying information (particularly your social security number) safe from neighbors, friends, and even family members (including children and parents), you're dramatically less likely to become a victim.

If, however, you've already been a victim or feel at risk of becoming a victim (going through divorce, had your social security number compromised, etc.), consider putting a freeze on your credit. This is more than just a fraud alert (which is free but not very effective). In freezing your accounts with each of the credit bureaus, you're given a PIN that will be required by the credit bureau EVERY time an organization wants to check your credit. You need to keep the PIN safe and secure. There may be a small fee from the credit bureaus for putting the freeze on your credit, but in the long run, it might be worth it.

By way of a reminder, a credit history (also known as a credit report, file, record, or background) is a compilation of your credit-related activities and can be compared to a teacher's or professor's grade book that records all of the homework, tests, quizzes, and projects done during the school year. On the other hand, a credit score (also known as a credit rating) is like the grade received at the end of each quarter or semester, except that a credit score can fluctuate daily because the information on your credit history is always changing (if nothing else, the accounts on your history are getting older each day, which is one factor in the score).

TODAY'S MONEY

Building Credit

Back in 2006, soon after we began to offer a monthly debtor education course for individuals and couples who were filing for bankruptcy, I had an "encounter" with a gentleman who got very angry with me and essentially called me a liar in front of the class. Here's how the scene went down:

We were discussing how to access our free credit report every twelve months through AnnualCreditReport.com (see steps below), and someone said they had heard that checking your credit can actually hurt your credit rating. I assured them that this was a myth and that checking your own credit had no impact on your FICO credit score.

At this point, this gentlemen flat out said that what I was saying was not true, and that he had personally been experiencing negative impacts on his FICO score by checking his credit. He was so insistent and convinced in his response, that I'll admit that I was at a loss for a moment.

When he was a little less than forthcoming about how he was checking his report regularly, I assured him and the rest of the class that FICO does not count against us any reports we pull ourselves. At the end of class, he told me in passing that he was paying a third-party company to pull his credit report, and that each month, his credit score was falling for the very reason of pulling it.

Lesson? Pulling your OWN credit report means that we pull it through AnnualCreditReport.com or directly from the credit bureaus, not through a third-party company like the one this gentleman was using. Apparently, they had not coded their "inquiry" properly with the credit bureaus so that each time they pulled this gentelman's report, his credit score went down a percent or so because it appeared that he was applying for a new loan every month. You also need to be aware that when your brother or sister-in-law that works at a bank or mortgage company pulls your "complimentary" credit report, it will likely have a similar negative impact.

Step-by-Step

Unless you're preparing to make a major purchase on credit soon (buying or refinancing a home or vehicle, starting a business, etc.) or you suspect that you may be the victim of identity theft, I usually suggest that you don't pull all three of your credit reports at once from AnnualCreditReport.com. Instead, consider rotating through them throughout the year, alphabetically as follows:

1. On or around January 1, go to AnnualCreditReport.com and pull your Equifax credit report.

2. On or around May 1, go to AnnualCreditReport.com and pull your Experian credit report.

3. On or around September 1, go to AnnualCreditReport.com and pull your TransUnion credit report.

Each time you pull a report, check it for accuracy. If there are errors, return to the credit bureau's home page soon (I suggest immediately) and follow the instructions to "dispute" information. There is a link to this option on the home page of each of the three credit bureaus.

For free help and education about your credit reports, contact a nonprofit credit counseling agency in your area. They should offer to go through your report with you, one-on-one, at no charge to explain to you what each item means. Check out the nonprofits at the three major industry trade associations: aiccca.org, accpros.org, and nfcc.org. Help and resources for identity theft victims is available at the Federal Trade Commission's page: www.consumer.ftc.gov/features/feature-0014-identity-theft.

FACTOID

The residents of approximately one in fourteen homes on the street where you live have been a victim of identity theft in the past twelve months. The majority of identity theft occurs on existing credit cards and other financial accounts, although the theft of personal information is growing. Thieves can use your personal information to open (and not pay for) utility accounts, receive medical services using your health insurance, file for an income tax return in your name, register for a firearm using your information, file for bankruptcy, or even provide your name and social security number during a law enforcement arrest!

Dos and Don'ts

▲ Do try to pull credit reports for all household members to minimize potential identity theft fall out.

▲ Do consider placing a fraud alert or, in case of actual ID theft, a credit freeze on your credit reports if you're worried about identity theft.

▲ Do dispute promptly any errors you find on your credit reports.

▽ Don't carry your social security card in your wallet.

▽ Don't leave personal information lying around where neighbors, visitors, or even your teenaged children or extended family members might find it.

▽ Don't forget to keep your children's social security numbers and personal information safe and secure. Thieves can use their identity to apply for loans, open utility accounts, and even rent a home.

14

MATCHING YOUR DEBT REPAYMENT PERSONALITY TO THE RIGHT DEPT REPAYMENT STRATEGY

The top question I hear as a financial education and credit counselor is, "What's the best way to pay off my debt?" This is not surprising. Debt is a massive financial migraine that can make daily life pretty miserable, and shining a lot of light on the problem can often make us feel nauseated.

I've heard and read lots of answers to this question. Shouldn't this have a simple response? Actually, there are plenty who want to complicate it. I'm not one of them. Here's my simple answer:

Most of us should organize our debts from the lowest balance to the highest balance and send extra payments to the debt on the top of the list while making minimum payments to the rest.

That's it! If you're okay with that, you can probably just skip to the next chapter. See you there!

Okay, so if you're still reading, you either want to know why or are among a portion of the population who feels like ripping the financial lungs out of anyone who adheres to such heresy. Rest assured, there is no need for that.

I am quite aware that the debt repayment method that makes the most financial sense is to send extra payments to our debt with the highest interest rate first. That seems like a no-brainer, but here's the thing: this is the accountant's method. It's meant for the financially disciplined who are self-motivated to pay off their debts. The problem is that most of us (though certainly not all) who get into a lot of debt don't accomplish that feat through disciplined and self-motivated efforts.

Instead, here's what I suggest for the majority of those wanting to pay off their debts: focus on paying off the smallest balance first. Whether your debt comes from the undisciplined use of credit, from not having an emergency savings fund at the time of a job loss, or from mild-to-moderate medical, vehicular, appliance, or other should-be-expecting-but-we-aren't-ready-for living expenses, this is the best method for most of us.

Here's my rationale behind this heresy. By focusing any extra payments you can make on the debt with the lowest balance first, you're most likely to get rid of your first creditor sooner than with the highest APR method. Also, each time you pay off a debt, it's one less monkey on your back and one more reason to stay motivated to repay all of your debt.

It's all about motivation.

If, on the other hand, you were to focus on the highest APR first, it could take a year or more to pay off, and all the while you're making minimum payments to some department store card with a $120 balance that just keeps hanging around and hanging around, even though you're making the requested monthly payment. A year later, thanks to the power of compound interest and the slippery slope of minimum payments, you're still making payments to the highest APR debt, and the department store card with a 19% APR still has two more monthly payments required before it's paid off. That's enough to dishearten anyone who feels trapped in an endless cycle of consumer debt.

So, yes, if you're the disciplined type, I wholeheartedly believe in sending extra payments to the debt with the highest interest rate. Most of us, though, will focus the extra payment (see the PowerCash chapter) on the debt with the lowest balance.

There are other methods I've read about for paying down debts that include everything from considering payment-to-balance ratios to cashing out a 401(k), from taking out a home equity loan to negotiating with the creditors, and more. I'm not going to say these methods don't work, because I know that they can and do for some people.

Here are my warnings to anyone considering some of these methods:

First, avoid anything that sounds or feels too complicated. It might work, but if you're not totally sold on it or don't completely understand it, you're probably setting yourself up for a financial downfall.

Second, don't drain cash from your emergency savings or from a retirement account to pay off credit cards and personal debts. At some point in the near future, you will probably need some cash (think appliance replacement, vehicle repair, back-to-school shopping, etc.), and if you've drained your savings account, you'll be tempted to put such purchases all on a credit card and end up right back where you started. If you borrow from your 401(k), you're putting your financial future at risk. 401(k)s are protected, to a large extent, even when filing for personal bankruptcy. Plus, I love how a student in one of my classes summed it up: "You can borrow money in just about any emergency, but not for retirement."

Third, borrowing money against the equity in your home is dangerous on multiple levels. To begin with, you're essentially using an asset that has real value in it and draining its value in order to pay for "unsecured" debt. Credit cards, collections, and many other types of debt are unsecured, which means there wasn't anything put up as collateral for the loan. Essentially, the creditor cannot come into your home and take anything if you default on the loan.

The two main types of "secured" debts are home loans and vehicle loans (many RV, boat, and motorcycle loans are also secured debts). The danger of using a home equity loan is that you're paying off an unsecured debt with additional secured debt against the home. The worst of it, though, is that 70 to 80 percent of households who use a home equity loan to pay off credit card debts will, within just a couple of years, run credit card balances right back up to their previous levels. So now they have credit card debt AND a home equity loan that put their home ownership at risk. Like borrowing against a 401(k) or draining a savings accounts, this option does not address the real problems many with credit card debt face: poor money management or insufficient emergency funds.

I would suggest considering calling the creditor up front. I don't typically suggest negotiating a settlement on the principal balance owed (see the chapter on third-party debt elimination assistance for a discussion on the effects of debt negotiations). However, it certainly can't hurt to ask creditors to lower their interest rates. They may refuse. It's up to each individual creditor and, to the same extent as with other customer service issues in life, up to their phone representatives what they can or will do for us. Having a history of on-time payments to that creditor, along with asking nicely, will certainly help. Threatening to transfer your balance to another credit card is also a tried-and-true way of extracting additional concessions from the credit card company.

However, if you're not dealing with credit card companies but rather collection agencies, you're likely to get pretty much nowhere with your requests. They have purchased your account from your previous creditor (for much less than what is actually owed on the account), so they now possess much the same rights as did the previous creditor. However, they typically want their money, and they want it now. My two suggestions for dealing with collection accounts are: (1) as soon as you get a collection notice, call the previous creditor and ask if they can bring your account "back in house," so that you can set up monthly payment arrangements with them or (2) consider offering less than the full balance owed to the collection agency.

The collection agency paid considerably less for the account than what is owed, so often anything above 20 or 30 percent of the original balance will be profit in their pockets. However, be aware that such negotiations will quite possibly result in more damage to your credit. Unless you get it in writing that they will not resell the amount they're forgiving, you could look forward to being contacted down the road by yet another collection agency that purchased the "forgiven" amount from the previous collection agency. Insist on getting any such agreement in writing.

TODAY'S MONEY

Matching Your Debt Repayment Strategy to Your Personality

A few years ago, I spoke at a continuing education lunch meeting of Certified Public Accountants where I shared information about credit counseling and how the industry's debt management programs could help their own clients. All seemed to be going well, with lots of head nodding in agreement about the benefits I was describing. Then, when I shared my opinion that, when paying off debts on our own, focusing extra resources on our debt with the lowest balance first is the best option for most consumers, it was as if I had blasphemed against the accounting gods. I knew such a statement was sacrilege for such a group, so I quickly reassured them that they were not included in my qualifier, "most consumers."

I then shared my belief that most consumers don't get into excessive consumer debt because they have an accountant's mentality and disposition. Nor, by contrast, do I believe that everyone in consumer debt arrived there by factors entirely within their control. Still, most of us trying to pay back our debts will benefit most from focusing on the smallest debt first rather than the debt with the highest interest rate.

Step-by-Step

Rate yourself from 1-5 (1 being "strongly disagree" and 5 being "strongly agree") using the following questions to help determine which debt repayment strategy is most appropriate for your personality.

Question 1: I am enrolled in a for-profit college.
(yes = 5, no = 1)

Question 2: I am unaware of what my credit score is.

Question 3: I am unemployed or underemployed.

Question 4: I bounce checks or overdraft my bank account frequently.

Question 5: I have used one of the following services in the past twelve months: payday loan, automobile title loan, rent-to-own, and/or check cashing.

Question 6: I often borrow money from family, friends, and/or my employer.

Question 7: I routinely max out my credit card(s). (If you have no credit card=5)

Question 8: I usually ignore my bank statements.

Question 9: I would have difficultly estimating my total debt (excluding mortgage) within $300.

Question 10: My age is: under 21 = 5; 21-25 = 4, 26-30 = 3; 66+ = 2; 31-65 = 1 (NOTE order of final two age groups)

If you scored a 20 or higher, you would probably benefit most from paying down your debts using the "Lowest Balance First" strategy. Otherwise, if you scored below 20, concentrating your extra payments on the debts with the highest interest rate would be most beneficial.

FOOD FOR THOUGHT

According to a Federal Reserve Bank of New York, the average student loan debt increased nearly 60% between 2005 and 2012. We now have more student loan debt than auto or credit card debt, and student loan debt is the only type of consumer debt to have increased since the economic recession began in 2008.

Dos and Don'ts

▲ Do write out a debt repayment strategy. The acts of writing down and regularly looking at this plan will provide a great deal of motivation.

▲ Do combine our debt repayment plan with a household spending plan. We can't dig ourselves out of debt if we continually debt ourselves deeper into it.

▲ Do start the debt repayment plan today, regardless of the chosen method.

▽ Don't put off debt repayment in hopes of finding a better method.

▽ Don't focus on our overall debt ,but on the one debt that we've identified as priority.

▽ Don't fear nonprofit credit counseling when we don't feel we can pay our debts on our own. If things get bad enough to consider bankruptcy, we'll need to speak with a nonprofit credit counselor anyway.

PART SIX

$

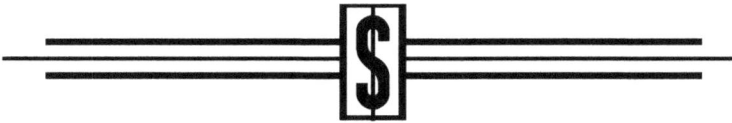

EVERYDAY DEBT REPAYMENT STRATEGIES

15

GOOD DEBT, SCHMOOD DEBT, BAD DEBT, SCHMAD DEBT

Being in the credit counseling industry and working for a company called, "Debt Reduction Services, Inc.," I get a lot of questions and hear a lot of stories about consumer debt. A large percentage of the classes I teach address the question of how to deal with excessive consumer debt.

Often, my students participating in discussions will ask me to identify good debt and bad debt. This is a long-established tradition, classifying debt as a dichotomy. Apparently, someone decided that money owed on a home for a postsecondary education or for a business is good debt. All other debt is bad debt. Unfortunately, as the great recession has recently demonstrated, led in part by the frightening home value correction in the housing market, not all mortgage debt is or should be considered good debt.

Additionally, there's the reality that student loan defaults rose from 12 to 15 percent over the past few years, according to FICO. That's not up 15 percent, but it is at 15 percent. That means that one in every six or seven student loans out there is in default. Could student loan debt, then, be the next bubble? With the economy only slowly recovering, and with jobs and wages stagnating, increased student loan debt will only serve to hamper recent graduates' ability to consume, consume, consume, which, as we've all been told over and over, drives 70 percent of the US economy.

As for business loan debt, it has always been the riskiest of the three. Many start-up businesses go out of business, and much of this business start-up or business acquisition debt is essentially personal debt. The current or soon-to-be-former business owner could end up in federal court filing for personal bankruptcy.

All this proves the traditional categorization of debt as either good or bad needs an overhaul. Here are my proposed classifications:

1. Potentially beneficial long-term debt

2. Practical short-term debt

3. Financially draining debt

No, it's not as catchy as "Good Debt, Bad Debt," but I think it's much more helpful.

Potentially beneficial, long-term debt basically replaces the term "good debt." However, adding the keywords of "potentially" and "long-term" would, or at least should, give those getting into such debt pause to consider the consequences of their actions. Yes, a mortgage is traditionally a better option financially than is rent. Yes, an undergraduate degree can double an individual's average lifetime earnings. And yes, owning a small business is the most common path to becoming a millionaire in this country. However, none of these loans comes with guarantees of success, and we, as borrowers, need to understand that better.

From here on out, let it be decreed that home loans, student loans, and business loans shall no longer be known, identified, or referred to as "good debt," but rather as "potentially beneficial, long-term debt."

To determine if a debt is potentially beneficial, you must be able to respond positively to at least one of the following questions: (1) Will it LIKELY increase, or at least not decrease, my net worth over time and (2) Will it LIKELY increase, or at least not decrease, my earning potential over my lifetime? If you answered no to either of these questions, the debt is not potentially beneficial.

Then we come to the smallest of the three categories: practical short-term debt. I define practical debt as debt taken on that incurs no interest, could be paid off immediately if necessary, and provides additional benefits such as security, convenience, and practicality that don't come from using cash or cash equivalents.

My main example of this includes using credit cards when traveling and then paying off that balance in full by its due date in order to avoid interest charges. The reason I specifically use a credit card and not a debit card does not have to do with the security features they both have (such as loss protection), nor with the convenience of them being accepted just about everywhere. I use a credit card when I'm traveling because it involves OPM, and OPM stands for Other People's Money. When I use a credit card, yes, I am technically taking out a loan every time I make a purchase, whether it's for a pizza or a night at a hotel. However, it's the credit card bank that is paying for those things up front, and if my wallet is lost or stolen and someone uses my credit card fraudulently, the thief is using OPM and not my money. Reporting the theft immediately means I'm often not liable for purchases incurred fraudulently or, at most, only up to fifty dollars.

If I were carrying a debit card, I could eventually recover that money spent by the thief, but it might take weeks. In the meantime, I'd be up a creek without means for purchasing a paddle.

A few words of warning, though. First, we should not use a credit card for purchases when we don't already have the money in the bank to cover the expenses we're incurring. And second, we need to estimate our expenses ahead of time, make sure they fit within our spending plans, and then stay within these spending limits. Honestly, and this comes from my own experience, the biggest threat to controlling spending when on vacation in particular is to make a realistic budget for meals and stick to it. It becomes far too easy to overspend on meals (and gifts and souvenirs and activities and . . .) when using a credit card without setting limits.

I classify all other debt not discussed above, and I mean ALL other debt, as financially draining. That includes car loans, any credit card debt carrying over from month to month, personal (signature) loans, definitely payday and title loans, and even home equity loans to pay down credit card debts.

With this revision of how to look at debt, I hope that it provides greater motivation to stop and reflect on the impact of debt, not just on your finances, but on your life. Some say that debt can be a powerful tool, usually referring to the purchase of home or other property. However, when used carelessly, power tools tend to break things and can make a mess of those who use them carelessly.

TODAY'S MONEY

Good Debt Schmood Debt

In spite of having been in the financial education business for a decade, I try not to be overconfident in my expressions of what we should or should not be doing with our money. Just about the time I believe I've figured out the best way of organizing a certain portion of my personal finances, someone shares an idea or asks an innocent question that throws a wrench into my money management construct, requiring me to revisit my financial views and principles.

One such experience occurred during a class a few miles from my office one morning a couple of years ago. The class and I were discussing good debt and bad debt, and I was confidently explaining that all debt, other than real estate, student, and business loans, is bad debt. Someone asked the usual question, "What about a car loan?" Oh, I was so ready for that question. I launched into explaining that cars, even most "classic" cars, are never worth more than what we pay for them (referring to their high rate of depreciation, the interest we pay on the loan, and the money we plow into maintenance and repairs over time).

I then got another common question, "What about needing a car to get to work?" Again, no problem. We discussed the idea that a vehicle's purpose is to get us from Point A to Point B and not to signify any social standing or provide additional luxuries. Consequently, we talked about buying used cars that were reliable yet affordable or using public transportation and ride sharing options.

Then came the comment that brought me a new perspective on car loans: "But what if the vehicle I purchase for my job or my business allows me to earn more money that the amount of interest and the depreciated value of the vehicle over time? Isn't that then 'good' debt?" Touché. They had me. I admit it.

If the vehicle we purchase allows us to earn more money than the amount we lose to interest and depreciation, then, yes, it could be considered "potentially beneficial" debt. And thank you, my friend, for helping me better understand my topic! Still, it's always important to remember that being in debt means that the lender has, to one extent or another, some control over our financial lives. That situation does not sit well with me, nor with most of you, I assume.

Step-by-Step

Student loan debt has exploded (or, according to many industry watchers, is about to burst like a bubble) in the United States, essentially doubling in the past decade. Here are a few simple steps to help us determine how much student loan debt is too much:

4. Estimate the median annual income of those working in the field of employment we're going to school for. Check out the Bureau of Labor Statistics at www.bls.gov/oes/current/oes_nat.htm or from the non-governmental site, www.salary.com.

5. Adjust the median income to take into account that we typically earn significantly less than the median wage early in our profession or career. Estimate our median income in the bottom 10% to 25% range of incomes in the field (found at these web sites).

6. Determine our estimated living expenses for our post-degree life. Don't forget to include savings, retirement contributions, vacations, gifts, philanthropy, furniture, appliances, transportation, housing, family, etc.

7. Use the repayment comparison calculator at http://studentaid.ed.gov/repay-loans/understand/plans/standard/comparison-calculator to estimate monthly student loan payment post-graduation. The average student loan for bachelor degree students, as of the writing of this book, is over $27,000. That works out to a monthly payment of over $300.

8. Add our estimated monthly student loan payment to our estimated living expenses to ensure that we can afford the debt.

If we can't afford the student loan monthly payment, we'll need to consider other options, including employment, grants and scholarships while in school, post graduation government work that can earn a forgiveness of our student loans, or even a different career choice that will still sustain our required lifestyle.

Statistics

According to the US Bureau of Labor Statistics, median earnings increase significantly for each educational degree we earn.

High School Diploma: 38% higher median income than
non-high school graduate
Associate's Degree: 20% higher than high school diploma
Bachelor's Degree: 36% higher than Associate's Degree
Master's Degree: 22% higher than Bachelor's Degree
Doctoral Degree: 25% higher than Master's Degree
A Professional Degree returns a 63% higher median
annual income than a Bachelor's Degree.

Dos and Don'ts

▲ Do consider all aspects of being debt free (including mortgage) and not just the financial advantages. Besides not paying interest, having no mortgage also means more freedom to move, sell, rent, etc.

▲ Do minimize the "practical" credit card debt when traveling by creating, carrying and sticking to a spending plan.

▲ Do keep debt to such a level that monthly minimum payments are well below the suggested 20% of our monthly net income. Of course, having NO debt payments would be even better.

▽ Don't swear off credit cards forever. If you ever want to purchase a home and need to borrow money for a mortgage, credit cards will be all but required to build your credit history.

▽ Don't max out student loans just because you qualify for the maximum amount.

▽ Don't get into business debt, if you're the entrepreneurial type, without major amounts of planning, professional guidance, and related experience.

16

THIRD-PARTY DEBT HELPERS
THE GOOD, THE BAD, AND THE RIDICULOUS

I am all for paying off debt on our own if we can. It often makes the most financial sense and allows us to fulfill our financial obligations independently. However, if the ideas in my previous chapter about paying off debts on your own are not feasible or practical, I'd like to present a realistic and fair overview of the options available when turning to third-party help.

First of all, I must disclose that I am and have been employed for nearly a decade by a nonprofit credit counseling agency, so please understand that what I say should be seen through those glasses. I will do my best to be honest, up front, and fair about each of these options, but bias comes into play for everyone, in spite of our best efforts.

I've identified types of organizations that offer essentially three types of services that, so they say, help us deal with our debt.

    ¢   First, we've got companies suggesting that we "reorganize" our debt in a manner that allows us to pay it off faster and with fewer fees and less interest.

    ¢   Then there are those who say they can help us pay off our debt at better terms, and lower fees and interest.

    ¢   Finally, there are those who exist to relieve us of our legal responsibility to repay our debts.

Generally, each has their time and place, although some offer greater benefits and others greater financial dangers as alternatives.

Let's start with those who encourage us to reorganize our debts. In general, they promote specific types of loans that might come with lower interest and fees. Examples would include those who suggest to pay down credit card debt, store card debt, and other such unsecured debts by borrowing against the equity in your home, against a retirement account (IRA, 401(k), 403(b), etc.), or use the cash value of a life insurance policy. I'm not going to say much about getting a consolidation loan from a financial institution other than even if we were to qualify for one, we'd likely end up paying life-threateningly high-interest rates. Nor am I going to address the "sport" of transferring debt from one credit card to another, since that's not technically paying down debt, just "repositioning" it. However, the other options mentioned do have their advantages and disadvantages to consider. On the plus side, the interest rates on most of these types of loans are negligible, especially when compared to credit cards and interest rates on other consumer debts. Some even have incentives, such as the current possibility of claiming home equity interest paid as a tax deduction.

Before we just delve into these options, let's remember a few words of caution: credit card debt once was tax deductible, until a law in the 1980s eliminated that benefit. Laws can change, so don't bet the farm on any tenuous supposition that Congress is not going to change the tax laws.

Furthermore, every single one of these options addresses the symptoms rather than the cause of the debt. If your credit card debt is a recent financial deviation directly tied to an extremely expensive life event (such as a medical emergency or long-term job loss), then these options might be a good idea. However, if your credit card and collections debts are long-term or habitual occurrences (something you're used to and have been living with for months, if not years), then these options are actually very financially dangerous, even poisonous.

Think about it. If you're used to living with credit card debt and paying interest every month, consider the temptation to borrow money against your home's equity, a retirement account, or a life insurance policy, and all of a sudden your credit cards have a zero balance? It's very likely that you'll be among the majority of people who take out such loans to pay down credit card debts. Within a year or two, 70 percent have charged their credit card balances right back to where they were previously. Now we're dealing with the same old credit card debt in addition to having placed the security of our home, retirement, or life insurance coverage in jeopardy.

I'll say it again, if you choose to go these routes, make sure to address the cause of your credit card debt first. Most household debt problems are caused less by income or interest and more by overspending.

The next group of third-party debt repayment options is fairly small. It consists mostly of nonprofit credit counseling agencies, although there are a handful of for-profit credit counseling agencies as well. Essentially, credit counseling agencies (CCAs) work to lower the interest rates on debts and to work out a repayment plan with creditors that involves more reasonable terms. The benefits would typically include lower interest rates, earlier pay offs, and ideally, lower monthly payments.

Keep in mind that I'm a credit counselor, but I'm trying to be as "real" as I can. Credit counseling isn't for everyone who has consumer debt. The ideal credit counseling client has high-interest credit card or collections debt, owes money on an old utility or cell phone account, has payday loans, probably has some medical debts (in collection), and might even have some back taxes or owe back child support. Legitimate credit counseling agencies should be able to work with virtually any debt except home and property loans, auto loans, other loans secured against assets, business debt, and any debts already claimed by a judgment in court. There should not be any minimum debt amount either, below which they won't agree to work. One of the first clients I worked with on the phone as a rookie counselor had just $800 of credit card debt. Because my company was able to bring her interest rate down significantly, it made sense for her to go with us.

Still, there are a few drawbacks to using a credit counselor, but they are not the ones many of my students think of. Many avoid using credit counselors because of the negative impact it will have on our credit. The reality is that FICO does not take credit counseling into account when computing our credit scores.[1] It used to, but that was back before 1999, when it became clear that participation in a credit counseling debt management program is not a reliable predictor of whether someone is more or less of a risk for defaulting on debts.

That said, and again I am trying to be as real as possible, there can be an indirect impact on credit scores because the accounts placed on the credit counselor's "debt management program" (or a DMP) are closed to any further use. By closing an account, this might bring the total balance closer to the amount of the total credit available, which can negatively affect a score. If you're maxed out on your cards, though, the impact will likely be negligible. Even so, the most important goal should be paying down debts at this point and not building credit. Still, by making on time payments to your creditors, even through a credit counseling agency, and by paying down and eventually paying off your consumer debts, your credit score will very likely go up.[2]

No, the main drawback of participating in a DMP involves the fees. Virtually all credit counseling agencies, nonprofit or not, will collect an enrollment fee if you choose to go on their DMP. There is no fee, or should not be one, for just meeting with a credit counselor, working out a household budget, and developing a debt elimination strategy.

Another fee is charged monthly and is often tied directly to either the number of accounts placed on the DMP or is calculated as a percentage of your monthly debt repayment through the credit counseling agency. Either way, every state has a cap on the monthly fee that can be charged. Most are in the fifty dollar range, though some are much less.

The one issue many in my classes think of as a drawback (but actually isn't one) is the impact that DMP participation has on a credit report. When people hear that creditors place a notation on their report while they're participating in a DMP, they freak out and start running for the hills. Fear not, people (and please come down from the hills)! That notation is actually a friend. Basically, it tells other creditors that you're in a DMP and that while you're working to pay off past consumer debts, they would very much appreciate it if other creditors would not open up any more accounts for you. Once leaving the DMP (whether or not you've completed it), the creditor usually takes that notation off your credit report automatically. If they don't, it's usually just a matter of submitting an error dispute with the credit bureaus to have the notation removed.

Finally, the last category of third-party debt counselors includes debt settlement companies and bankruptcy attorneys. Both strive, to one degree or another, to help get you out of your responsibility (moral or legal) to pay some or all of your debts.

I'll start with debt settlement companies. I'll be honest: I'm not a big fan of the industry. Take this with a grain of salt, I guess, coming from a credit counselor, but there are just way too many bad actors in the industry for my taste right now. Maybe the Consumer

Financial Protection Bureau can get them to clean up their collective act and weed out the chaff from the tares, but for now, I would never suggest that anyone look up a debt settlement company on the Internet and work with them. Get a referral from someone you trust, including a credit counselor, the Better Business Bureau, or family or friends who have used the program.

Besides, debt settlement companies usually offer to do what you can already do for yourself (and you won't charge yourself their hefty fees). Unlike credit counseling that negotiates for better interest rates (which, by the way, you can also do with an individual creditor, but when the creditor knows that other lenders are involved, they actually prefer that you go with a credit counseling agency), debt settlement companies (DSCs) ask you to stop paying your creditors altogether and send a monthly payment instead to the DSC, who will "hang onto it" in a trust fund (if you're working with a legitimate company) until you have paid them enough for them to feel comfortable approaching your creditor to offer less that the current balance. If accepted, yeah, you have paid the creditor significantly less than what you owed them. Don't forget, though, that you have also been paying each month to a company that will often take a debt balance fee, a monthly administrative fee, a negotiation fee, an amount forgiven fee, and several other fees that can easily add another 15 to 25 percent of the original amount owed.

Additionally, the creditor will, most likely, at the beginning of the next calendar year, send you a 1099-C tax form, indicating how much money they "gave" you that year by forgiving a portion of your debt. The IRS, in turn, then usually gets interested in that "forgiven" amount because it is usually considered taxable income. That means that you get to pay taxes on that amount. Yahoo! Along with the DSC fees, you end up paying somewhere between 70 and 90 percent (or more) of the original balance. And that's the good scenario where you aren't sued by the creditor during the time of sending payments to the DSC or have your wages garnished by that creditor (not to mention other creditors in line to sue and garnish as well).

In the end, though, the real problem I have with most of these organizations is their overall ineffectiveness. As an industry, they report a rosy success rate of somewhere in the 30–40 percent range. Reports I give more credence to put their success rate in the single digit range. It doesn't help that we, as a credit counseling agency, see more than our share of clients coming into our offices and describing the nightmare they've had with a DSC that took all of their money and delivered no benefit to them in the end. By the time these individuals come to see us, their finances are in such bad shape that we can often do no more than refer them to a bankruptcy attorney.

Which brings us to the last option: bankruptcy. Bankruptcy is a legal action filed in federal court (not with a creditor or a bank as many might think). It is meant to protect us (the debtor) from an eternity of indebtedness following situations in our lives that produce an overwhelming amount of debt. Bankruptcy is particularly appropriate for households that want to protect a home that could be foreclosed on.

The one positive about going through a bankruptcy is the concept that the debtor gets a "fresh start" on their financial life. Whether or not this is true with each filer is not easy to tell. Many debts, including 97 to 98 percent of student loans and just about anything else owed to or through the government is next to impossible to get rid of (think child support, recent taxes, restitution, and fines, etc.).

Still, bankruptcy exists for a reason, and the days of bankruptcy filers hearing their names shouted from the rooftops (okay, that never actually happened, at least not that I'm aware of) are fading into the past. A few newspapers still publish the names of individuals in their areas who have recently filed for bankruptcy, but the social stigma is less than it used to be. That doesn't mean it's easy or fun to file for bankruptcy. Of the thousands of people who have come through my bankruptcy classes, I don't recall any of them ever saying they enjoyed the process.

The drawbacks to bankruptcy are significant but should not dissuade those in true need of help. The drawbacks start with court fees that are typically hundreds of dollars, plus attorney fees that range from hundreds to thousands of dollars, depending upon where we live and how complex our financial situation is. Bankruptcy is also the single most damaging action we can have on our credit. It's worse than foreclosure, short sales, and collection accounts and can reasonably be expected to drop our credit score about 25 percent.

Still, the further in the past the bankruptcy is, the less it damages our credit, until "poof!" after ten years, it's no longer on our credit reports at all (or shouldn't be—it's time to submit an error dispute if it is). I've met couples who have gone through my bankruptcy class and, two years later, have recovered enough, credit-wise, that they are able to qualify for a really good interest rate on a new home.

So don't despair. Bankruptcy is there if you need it. It's not the end of the world. Life changing? Certainly! Life ending? Of course not.

TODAY'S MONEY

When It Comes to Debt, Act Early

I happened to be walking by the front desk at work one day last year when a senior couple walked in, all but frantic about their debt situation. They felt overwhelmed by some medical and other debts they had, so they responded to an ad promising to help them get rid of their debts by only having to pay half of what they owed. The company may even have been a nonprofit debt settlement company. The company's representatives called themselves debt counselors and were nice and obliging on the phone. This couple set up a monthly payment that went to the company and then, at the urging of the company, sent letters to all of their creditors asking them not to contact them anymore.

It had been eight months since those initial phone conversations, and they had just found out that the company had gone out of business and had no money left in their account to return to this couple. All of that money was essentially flushed down the toilet.

The couple came to us hoping we could help. Eight months prior, we likely could have, but their debts had grown so large, and it had been so long since their creditors had received a payment from the couple, they were no longer willing to work with us. Unfortunately, the couple's only option left was to file for bankruptcy.

It's frustrating when we meet with such couples and individuals in their golden years who have been given terrible advice or who have just plain been scammed out of their nest egg.

Again, take this from a credit counselor's point of view, but the sooner an individual or couple can meet with a credit counselor (for which there should never be a fee), the sooner they can receive proper advice and guidance on the practical and realistic options available to them. To find a nonprofit credit counseling agency approved by the US Department of Justice, see http://www.justice.gov/ust/eo/bapcpa/ccde/cc_approved.htm.

Step-by-Step Out of Debt

Figure out which debt repayment option is appropriate for your situation by answering the following simple questions:

¢ Do you have sufficient income and assets you can use to meet (or come close to meeting) monthly debt obligations? If yes, continue. If no, consider bankruptcy, particularly if there is no near-term prospect of improving your income.

¢ Do you currently, or within the next three to four months, have access to enough income or assets to pay off about half of the debt that is causing trouble? If yes, consider debt settlement (on your own before hiring an expensive service). If no, continue.

¢ Do you have regular income that is barely or not quite enough to meet your monthly debt payments? If yes, then meet with a licensed credit counseling agency. If no, you may be in a situation to repay your debts on your own or through a nonprofit credit counselor.

QUOTE

Some help us eliminate debt. Some want us to pay it.
Still others more likely contribute to it.
—Todd

Dos and Don'ts

▲ Do consider all of your options.

▲ Do seek help early. The longer you wait when your finances are dire, the fewer options you will have.

▲ Do your research on the third-party company you're considering working with. Check them out with the Better Business Bureau (bbb.org) and consider contacting the state's attorney general's office about the organization.

▲ Do check with your local state authority (finance or banking department, secretary of state, etc.) to ensure that any third-party company you work with is duly registered and in good standing.

▽ Don't touch your retirement funds.

▽ Don't simply steal from Peter to pay Paul (transfer debt from one card or account to another).

▽ Don't use your assets (equity) to pay down unsecured debts (credit cards, store cards, etc.) without addressing the root cause of your debt (overspending, recurring medical bills, extended job loss).

17

MAY THE POWERCASH BE WITH YOU!

When it comes to saving money, the first mistake we can make is to say (and actually believe) that whatever we have left over at the end of the month will go into our savings account. Come on, folks, let's be honest. There is always more month left over at the end of our money than vice versa. The worst part about this feeble attempt to put money aside is that we NEVER succeed, so we assume that our savings problem is the supposed fact that we don't have enough money to save. It is my pleasure at this time to attempt to disabuse anyone still clinging to such an excuse of this false belief.

Let's say, for argument's sake, we didn't have enough money. How much would be enough? An extra $5,000 a year? An extra $25,000? Seriously, how much do we need before we can say that we have enough to start saving a few extra bucks a month?

No matter what our income, the reality is that saving is a commitment, not an amount (sound familiar?). Say it with me:

Saving is a commitment, not an amount.

Chew on this tidbit: when I go into middle school classrooms, I love to start off with this series of questions:

1. If I were to give you $1, what would you spend it on in the next sixty minutes?

2. How about $10 in the next sixty minutes?

3. What about $100 by the end of the day?

4. $1,000 by the end of the day?

5. $10,000 by tomorrow night?

6. $100,000 by the end of the week?

Not surprisingly, each class of twelve- and thirteen-year-old kids has no problem in the least coming up with multiple ways to spend all of that money in a short period of time. So if a twelve- or thirteen-year-old can spend $100,000 within a week, we, as clever adults, should also be able to find multiple ways to spend any amount of money thrown at us. And when I say "any," I mean "any."

As proof, think about the last time you got a raise in your household income or a new job that paid more money. I'd bet you thought, "At last, I'm going to be making enough to finally start saving some money for the future!" Then what happened? Two months after the raise or starting a new job, you realized you still weren't making enough money to put anything into a savings account.

The reason is not because you weren't making enough, and it wasn't because you were moved to a higher tax bracket. It had everything to do with the fact that you let human nature run its course. And human nature says, plain and simple:

The more money we make, the more money we spend.

It's not just human nature, either. Doesn't the federal government (regardless of the party in power) prove the same point that throwing more money at a problem is not necessarily the answer?

Saving is a commitment, not an amount.

Let's be honest. The reason most of us haven't started saving is because we believe it will be too financially painful to take money out of our household cash flow and park it in a savings account where it's "not being used."

Here's where the concept of PowerCash comes in. The PowerCash method allows a family (based upon the 2011 median household income in the United States of $50,054 according to the US Census Bureau) to typically save anywhere from $50 to $150 per month without much noticeable difference in lifestyle.

Instead of deciding upon a set percentage to save every month on an entire income, the PowerCash method takes 10 percent of only certain "controllable" household expenses. These include groceries, entertainment, gasoline, gift giving, vacations, and dining out, among others. If the household typically spends $500 per month on groceries, 10 percent of the groceries expenses alone would become $50 in PowerCash.

For the purposes of Everyday Savings in this book, PowerCash can be used to kick-start your savings habit. For it to be effective, though, you absolutely must remove your PowerCash from a checking account or other place where you stash your cash and place it directly into a savings account(s). Otherwise, if you're tempted to say, "I'll put into savings whatever I've got left at the end of the month," you're doomed to not save anything.

On the other hand, if you remove the savings amount from your checking account as soon as the money comes in, you will automatically adjust your spending for the rest of the month.

The "power" of PowerCash comes in handy when talking about accelerating your debt repayment strategy or about boosting retirement and long-term savings plans.

After experiencing the liberating power of using the PowerCash in your own household, be sure to share your story (check out oureverydaymoney.wordpress.com for such opportunities) and, more importantly, with those you care about. Your success can motivate others to make similar powerful and positive changes in their own finances.

TODAY'S MONEY

Where Did It All Go?

If I were to sit down one-on-one with just about any of my students and ask them to account for all the money they spent during the previous month, they would, as with most of us, only be able to remember where about 80 percent of their money went. That doesn't automatically mean that they were spending the other 20 percent frivolously. Often this 20 percent includes periodic or one-time purchases that are easily forgotten.

However, the consistency of this figure indicates, in spite of the common feeling that there is no wriggle room in monthly budgets, there often is. The PowerCash principle helps you take advantage of some of the "free" money (available, not *gratis*) to more quickly realize your financial goals.

Step-by-Step

¢   Add up your average month expenses for groceries, gift giving, vacation and travel, dining out, entertainment (movies, songs, video games, etc.), and any other expense that both varies each month and has no specific "bill due" date.

¢   Multiply the amount from Step 1 by 10 percent (x .1). This is your PowerCash.

¢   Remove your PowerCash from your checking account immediately after payday and send it to the priority account you've identified (usually a debt, a savings, or an investment account).

FACTOID

According to a 2012 Gallup poll, the average household in the United States spends around $150 per person per month on groceries.[1] The median expense on groceries was actually just $125 per person per month, indicating that those who spend more usually spend a lot more. Interestingly, and contrary to what we typically hear in the media and "feel" in our gut, we are actually spending less as a percentage of our household income than we have since the survey began back in 1943!

What this all means is that if we have a household of three, we likely spend $375 per month on groceries, and we should be able to come up with $37.50 of PowerCash that can accelerate savings, retirement, or debt elimination plans.

Dos and Don'ts

▲ Do keep a record of your monthly expenses by category (receipts, Mint.com, Quicken, spreadsheet, etc.).

▲ Do put your PowerCash on autopilot by scheduling automatic transfers from checking to savings or by scheduling automatic bill payments to debts for the day after payday.

▲ Do apply the PowerCash (10 percent) principle to any sudden windfalls such as income tax refunds, inheritances, escrow overpayment refunds, etc.

▽ Don't include utilities, rent, mortgage, or insurance premiums in your PowerCash calculations.

▽ Don't stop using the PowerCash principle after paying off debts, since it's also great for building savings and boosting investments.

▽ Don't be shy about sharing your progress with family, friends, and social networks. The PowerCash Principle is too, well, *powerful* to keep to yourself.

PART SEVEN

S

EVERYDAY SAVINGS

18

EXPECTING THE FINANCIALLY UNEXPECTED

Seemingly, the most complex questions to ask about savings, but ones that can be answered fairly, directly, and precisely, have to do with what we should be saving for and how much we should be saving.

Initially, the commitment to save is more important than the amount. As we begin to realize that we can save for multiple medium- to long-term goals, we will want to sit down and figure out both the "what" to save for and the "how much" we will need to be saving for each.

The alternative to saving for these short- to medium-term needs should be unspeakable. What are the options for a household when something like the fridge dies (by the way, on average after about seventeen years)? To purchase a new fridge for, let's say, $1,000, if the money is not in savings already, the household will likely turn to one of the following painful budgeting nightmares (in order of least helpful to most deadly):

¢ Purchasing a new fridge using store credit at an appliance and furniture store, which can easily reach into the mid to upper 20% APR range. The only upside to this over the credit card options explained below is that you'll typically need to make a set monthly payment, which means that it will usually be paid off in one to two years.

¢ Purchasing the new fridge on a credit card and paying an average interest rate of 15% APR or so on the $1,000 for the next five to ten years until that is paid off.

¢ Taking out a credit card cash advance at 20% or more APR (for which there is no grace period without interest, by the way) and paying interest for the next ten years or so.

¢ Borrowing from a retirement plan may seem like a good idea because the repayment terms appear fairly friendly, but remember that once that money is out of your retirement account, it's no longer working to get you ready for retirement. Taking out $1,000 could very well push your retirement date back anywhere from one month to half a year or more.

¢ Borrowing against your home's equity might carry a fairly low interest rate and provide some tax incentives, but you've essentially placed your home in jeopardy. If you can't make the new payment, for whatever reason, you could lose your home because you borrowed money for a fridge.

¢ Renting to own a fridge might see like a smart idea. After all, the advertised forty-five-dollar payments seem fairly reasonable, right? Be aware, though, that these payments are likely weekly, not monthly payments. If you go this route and actually DO end up making all of the required weekly payments (without missing one, since that could reset the terms or end up getting the fridge repossessed), you'll most likely have paid $2,000 to $3,000 for a fridge now worth just $500 or so. That is equivalent to a 200% to 500% APR on a credit card.

¢ Turning to payday lenders to take out a loan of $1,000 (or more likely going to two payday lenders for two $500 loans because many states restrict a payday loan to a $500 maximum), you'd likely end up having to pay back $1,150 to $1,250 within two weeks. However, since you're unlikely to have that kind of money ready to pay back in just two weeks, you'll do a "roll over" and pay just the payday loan fees of $150 to $250, which literally "buys" us another two weeks in order to pay off the debt.

After rolling it over three times (plus the fee from the original loan term period), you'll already have paid $600 to $1,000 in fees and STILL owe the original $1,000 borrowed. It'll now be just two months down the road from having purchased the new fridge, and you'll have almost doubled the cost of that fridge. That is equivalent to APRs of 400% to 650%. There's a very real reason why I say that this option brings up the rear (in the literal and very figurative sense of the expression).

So, figuring out the "what else" to save for, besides a fridge, is as easy as walking through your home (and garage and backyard) and looking for anything that will eventually wear out or break and will require more than one hundred dollars to replace. After writing them down, use the form provided within this book (or one similar to it) to figure out how much to save each month for each item. Essentially, you subtract the item's current age in years from its life expectancy and multiply that by twelve to figure out how many more months to reasonably expect the item to last. Then, divide the estimated replacement cost by the number of months left to figure out how much money each month you should be saving. That's it!

TODAY'S MONEY

Planning Ahead for the Worst

Refrigerators die. That's a sad fact of life. We should know this. We should expect our fridge to die some day. We just hope it's not today . . . or tomorrow . . . or next week. All too often, we don't prepare for what we know will eventually happen.

One hundred people were surveyed. The top five answers were given for the following question: "When your fridge dies, what will you do?"

"Don't replace it, but instead, I'll buy several large coolers to store my food in and will buy a couple of bags of ice each day."

"Purchase a new fridge with money I've been saving for the past ten years or so. That way, I can haggle on the price and know that I'm getting a good deal."

"Use my credit card to buy a new one and pay 16% interest on that fridge for the next five years."

"Apply for store credit and use the 'no interest–same as cash' option. Unfortunately, if I don't make at least my minimum payment on time every month AND if I don't pay it off 100% by the end of the term, the store will go back to day one of the loan and add interest at something like 25% APR."

"Go to a payday lender to borrow $500 for the next two weeks. I'll use that money to buy a used fridge that, I hope, will last more than a couple of years. Then, two weeks from now, I'll roll over those loans for another two weeks by paying only the fee (about 20 percent, or $200). Since I'm an average person, within the next twelve months, I'll have taken out eight other payday loans, paying an annualized interest rate of over 500%."

Can you place them in order of most expensive to least expensive?

Step-by-Step

Use the following table with Life Expectancies for Household Appliances to determine how much to save each month to be reasonably prepared when they need to be replaced. Apply the same principle to other future expenses that can be predicted.

	Refrigerator	Washer	Drier	Dishwasher	Microwave	Furnace	Central Air Conditioner	Water Heater	Bread Machine	TV	Computer	Vehicle	Smart Phone	Carpeting	Garage Door Opener
Life Expectancies (yrs)	17	13	14	10	11	18	15	11-13	3-5	10-15	5-10	12	2-5	11	10
Current Age (yrs)															
= Years Left															
x 12 Months															
= Months Left															
Replacement Cost															
÷ Months Left															
= $ ÷ Mo To Save															

Dos and Don'ts

▲ Do take an inventory of your home appliances and furniture BEFORE starting this project.

▲ Do set up a separate savings account to deposit appliance and furniture money into automatically each month.

▲ Do a simple Internet search for the item that will need to be replaced, plus its "life expectancy" (e.g., life expectancy of trampoline).

▽ Don't forget the furnace, A/C, and sprinkler system.

▽ Don't justify not saving by saying it all adds up to too much money . . . It's cheaper to save now than to pay and pay and pay later.

▽ Don't wait another month.

QUOTE

"Spare and have is better than spend and crave."

—Benjamin Franklin

19

SIMPLIFIED SAVINGS SYSTEMS

"I am a savings raider. There, I've said it. Hello, my name is Todd, and I'm a savings raider." ("Hi, Todd" heard in the background).

I am. From some of my earliest memories, through college and into my young adulthood when I saw a large portion of my weekly allowance money going into a bank savings pouch, I have always found it challenging to resist the urge to withdraw my money from savings once it reached an amount I considered, well, "considerable." I recall several periods when I would put some money from every paycheck into my savings account, watch it grow, and then withdraw it to go on a spending spree.

The fact that I had one savings account that was tied directly to my checking account made it easy to transfer money into it and out of it. For many of us, this ease of transfer is both the blessing and the curse of savings accounts.

I've mentioned the curse already—that it's too easy to transfer money back out of savings accounts. Let's address how to overcome this curse and turn it into a blessing.

To begin with, you need to establish a separate savings account for each of your savings goals. If the bank or credit union says to pay a monthly fee for each additional savings account or to keep a specified minimum balance in each, you should tell them to take a hike, and then consider taking your money to another bank or credit union. Multiple savings accounts may seem to bring more complexity to your finances than you may prefer, but in the long run, it will help to simplify and support your savings strategies.

One of the problems many households have when it comes to savings is that there is one savings account for all of their short-term, medium-term, and emergency needs. In the previous chapter, we figured out how to reasonably prepare for predictable expenses, even if they were unexpected, by turning periodic expenses into small, fixed savings transfers each month. If, however, all of these small savings transfers are going into one single, lone, solitary savings account for the entire household, that account will likely grow pretty significantly in a short period of time.

There are two challenges this scenario presents us with. First, when savings raiders like me see such significant balances in their accounts, they are tempted to spend it on wants and immediate impulses. Referring to the account as just a "savings account" is too generic to overcome these impulses. By generic, I mean that the savings account is seen just as a savings account and is not connected psychologically or emotionally with the goals behind the account. When logging in to an online account or looking at the savings account statement, it's simply referred to as "Savings" or as "Savings 001."

To turn this generic and somewhat meaningless account into something more significant, most banks and credit unions allow you to "name" it. When you log in to your online account, this option is found under account preferences or settings. For example, if you are building "Savings 004" specifically for a family vacation, why not name it such? I don't mean naming it, "Family Vacation." Still too generic. I mean, give it the name of where you want to take the family on vacation. Is it a special place or activity or park? Is it a family member you want to visit? Trust me. Giving it such a specific name will make savings raiders like me pause and think more than twice before dipping into it for trivial expenses.

You should do the same for all of your savings accounts. Be specific. What brand and color of washer and dryer or fridge are you saving for? What do you want to do with your yard fund? What type of equipment do you want to purchase with your hobby or electronics or household fund? The more specific, the more meaningful (and motivational) the account will be.

A sure way to help savings raiders minimize the chances of dipping into a savings account prematurely (and for the wrong reasons) is to make it as inconvenient as possible to do so. I like the idea of finding a second financial institution just for short-term and mid-term savings accounts. Look around your area and consider finding a bank or credit union that only has one branch or that at least doesn't have a branch anywhere near your home, office, or an area you regularly drive through or visit. Ideally, find one that's NOT open on Saturdays or after your normal work shift ends. If possible, it shouldn't have a drive-through lane either.

When you open up these savings account(s), do NOT request an ATM card or debit card tied to the account. In fact, ask them specifically NOT to send any such card. Again, the idea is to make it as inconvenient as possible to access your funds. The suggestions above make it inconvenient with regards to time, location, and physical access.

Finally, set up a direct deposit of your fixed savings transfer funds into the accounts at this new institution. Do this by setting up the direct deposit from your paycheck at your place of employment, or set up a direct transfer from your main checking account. If your checking account comes with bill pay, simply set up an automatic bill pay each month, for example, to be sent to your account number at the second savings institution.

The last option to make savings raiding as inconvenient as possible is to open up an online savings account. There are a number of banks that offer online banking ONLY. For such accounts, it might take a couple of days to transfer any money back into your checking account, giving you time to reconsider any unplanned purchases. Some online banks, like the one that runs SmartyPig.com, offer the option to create multiple savings goals WITHIN a single online savings account. These types of services can be powerful goal-setting and achieving tools for those who have a tendency to reach too quickly for their saved money in times of want rather than in times of need.

Use one or more or all of the above suggestions to make your savings habit part of your permanent financial behavior rather than some phantasmic financial fantasy.

TODAY'S MONEY

Simplified Saving

My wife and I love the Harry Potter series of books and movies almost as much as we enjoy Disney's theme parks. So when Universal Studios Orlando opened the Wizarding World of Harry Potter in 2010, we realized that we had to go. We've had other vacations since, but once we set the goal of going, we set up a vacation savings account. We used the notion of naming our account so that it is much more motivating than "Savings 004." The online bank we're using to save for this vacation (which we're finally taking this year with our two youngest) actually displays our savings as "Hogwarts Galleons and Magic Money."

If you were a savings raider, wouldn't you be less likely to "steal" from Hogwarts and Mickey than you would from an account named "Savings 004?" I would, and I am.

Step-by-Step

Use one or more of the following steps to set up automatic transfers from your main checking account to your savings accounts, whether they be at the same institution as your checking account, at a separate institution, or at an online-only institution:

1. Through your financial institution's online account center, set up transfers from your checking account to your savings account(s) to happen on the same day of the month, every month.

2. Use your financial institution's bill pay to send money from your checking account automatically on the same day of each month to a savings account at a different institution. Normally, you'll just need the routing and account num-

bers where the savings are held. If you're not sure of the routing number, websites like RoutingNumbers.com and FindRoutingNumbers.com can help.

3. If you have a separate online bank for savings, the bank will offer an option to have your deposits taken electronically from your main checking account.

Dos and Don'ts

▲ Do use an FDIC- or NCUA-insured financial institution for your savings (emergency and short-term accounts).

▲ Do use the FDIC's Electronic Deposit Insurance Estimator at www.fdic.gov/edie or the NCUA's Electronic Share Insurance Calculator at http://webapps.ncua.gov/ins to determine how much and how safe your deposits are.

▲ Do save. No matter what. Save! Except when you're unemployed with no income, there will never be a better time to start saving than today.

▽ Don't keep tens of thousands of dollars in a savings account where it will currently earn less than 1% APY (unless you're retired or otherwise need absolutely no risk in your finances). Talk to a financial adviser if you have this much money in a savings account.

▽ Don't open accounts in so many financial institutions that you lose track of them.

▽ Don't forget to review and balance your savings statements regularly. Many people don't realize that they should be balancing their savings accounts just as their checking accounts.

FACTOID

As of March 2013, the Federal Deposit Insurance Corporation listed 971 savings institutions in the United States. In a 2012 report, Bankrate.com said there were an additional 7,351 credit unions at the end of 2011.

PART EIGHT

$

EVERYDAY WASTE MANAGEMENT

20

WE'VE ALL GOT OUR OWN "DOLLAR DUMPS"

Dump yards. Garbage dumps. Refuse Disposal Sites. Sanitary land-fills. Whatever the name or the euphemism, they refer to the physical location where our trash is destined to land. As adults, we associate the dump with dirt, waste, and smell, but as a kid, it was an exciting experience to visit the dump with my dad or my older brothers. One person's trash is another kid's treasure (that was back in the day when we could get out and rummage through the piles and take home some new-to-us, broken-down toy). Ah, those were the days!

Financially speaking, we all visit "Dollar Dumps" today, some of us more frequently than others. A Dollar Dump is a place where we go to throw away our money, usually on something of little to no value, or on something that we could do or make for ourselves for less.

Like the dumps of my youth, there's often a thrill associated with to-day's Dollar Dumps, albeit a not-so-cheap-thrill. And like the dumps of my youth, Dollar Dumps can serve a purpose, although usually as an attempt to deal with emotional or psychological needs and desires (some superficial, others profound) that are either unfulfilled or appear out of reach. However, we should be extraordinarily careful not to let them drain our wallets and stink up household finances.

Where are these Dollar Dumps? We all have our own Dollar Dump that we visit, sometimes daily, sometimes weekly, or less frequently.

Anyone who says they don't waste money is likely trying to fool others and usually succeeding at fooling themselves.

Here are a few of the more common Dollar Dumps that have a negative impact, which needs to be minimized in our finances:

¢ Gourmet coffee shops: a $4.50 latte each morning on our way to work adds up to over $1,100 each year. If money's tight, we could drop this dump for a home brew from a high-end machine and save $500 to $1,000 in just the first year alone (not counting the extra driving for not having to go out of our way to get to the coffee shop).

¢ Lunch out: anyone who eats out for lunch every workday is likely to be dropping an average of $6.50 each time. Drinks, candy bars from vending machines, weekly lottery tickets... that adds up. For some, budget busters like these may not be a daily thing but are built into our finances "by default" or expectation. We pay for them monthly and don't stop to think how much they add up to over a year's time. Larger Dollar Dumps might include paying for cable or satellite television, expensive cell phone services, car detailing or washing, yard or lawn service, or even housecleaning help. Grabbing one item from the vending machine every weekday, at a dollar a pop, means we're spending five dollars a week on what is likely junk food. That's over twenty dollars a month and over $250 a year on that stuff. Double that figure if we're buying both a candy bar AND a soft drink. So the next time someone says that playing the lottery is about the same as investing in the stock market, suggest that such a comparison is like saying moonlight is as bright at sunshine. Yes, the difference is night and day.

TODAY'S MONEY

Don't Dump that Dollar!

Many financial coaches and experts preach the dangers of habitual small dollar purchases. I've been doing this for a decade myself. Such Dollar Dumps can strongly disrupt a household spending plan. That said, I am not advocating that we eliminate 100 percent of such purchases, although I do believe that virtually all American households have one or more Dollar Dumps that we should try to minimize.

Every household deals with different Dollar Dumps. From my own observations over the past decade, I find that the higher our income, the more they add up. For many of my students who are unemployed or struggle to pay living expenses, their Dollar Dumps tend to be items like a daily can of Coke or an energy drink. At three dollars a bottle or large can, five of these energy drinks a week adds up to $750 or more a year. For someone living on Social Security disability, that could be as much as 5 percent of their annual income. Add in four lottery tickets a week and we're talking about nearly 9 percent of their annual income.

Lest we think that lower-income households have a monopoly on Dollar Dumping, I notice that households with incomes near or just above the median income tend to dump dollars on things like daily coffee at gourmet shops and buying more meals at fast-food restaurants once, if not twice, a week. Together, these Dollar Dumps could add up to over 7 percent of the annual net income of a four-member household. Add in purchases of video games and the paraphernalia that come with them, and we could easy shoot past 10 percent.

Higher-income households (those, I estimate, with annual incomes 50 percent or higher than the national median household income) appear to dump their dollars at nicer restaurants, at cultural events, on home furnishings, or on vehicle leases.

I'm not saying that all low-income households dump dollars on Coke, that medium income households eat out at McDonald's a lot, or that high-income households eat at five-star restaurants regularly. These are just general observations I've made.

A point I make in my classes is that I would care less about our Dollar Dumps if so many of us weren't living paycheck-to-paycheck or worse. That's why I suggest finding ways to minimize these Dumps and their impact on our household finances.

Step-by-Step

Here are some ideas for minimizing our Dollar Dumps:

¢ Instead of eating out for lunch every day, take a bag lunch two to three times each week. You'll likely save $500 to $750 each year.

¢ Rather than hitting the vending machine each day for a soft drink, energy drink, or even juice, buy it in bulk and take one to work each day. You'll save $300 to $500 annually.

¢ Rather than dump $7,800 into lottery tickets over the next fifteen years and get nothing in return (come on, people, the odds are worse than astronomical that you'll win any significant amount), you have more than a 50/50 chance of having nearly $17,000 in a traditional IRA or 401(k) if you put the same amount in regularly. That's more than double your investment!

¢ Even buying a $100 espresso/latte machine can save $500 a year or so over going to the gourmet coffee shop.

¢ Instead of paying $110 or more each month for the premium sports TV package (usually to watch one game a week for the most part), why not invite yourself over to your best friend's home and offer to bring $15 worth of food? If you did that weekly (which you probably wouldn't), you'd still save over $500 annually. Plus, you're not stuck vacuuming the "sports den" afterwards!

FACTOID

According the Bureau of Labor Statistics, Americans spend an average of nearly 1 percent of their annual income on alcohol, 5.7 percent on dining out, and 1.9 percent on television, cable, and music. Amazingly, we only spend 3 percent of our annual income at doctors' offices. For all of our collective groaning and complaining about the skyrocketing cost of health care in this country, we spend almost three times as much on discretionary Dollar Dumps.

Dos and Don'ts

▲ Do track your Dollar Dumps for a month (keep tissue close by).

▲ Do make a plan to minimize your Dollar Dumps.

▲ Do write down something positive or motivating that you'd like to do with any Dollar Dump money saved.

▲ Do share your Dollar Dump plan with a family member or close friend for support.

▽ Don't think that addressing your Dollar Dumps will solve the rest of your financial challenges.

▽ Don't think that you are above having Dollar Dumps, regardless of your education or income.

▽ Don't start tomorrow; start today, since every day you wait means more money out of your pocket.

21

NOT ALL EXPENSES WERE CREATED EQUAL

Does a good mystery grab your attention? Are you one who loves watching for clues and figuring out the backstory of the mystery before the end of the book or show? Well, how about solving some of the deep financial mysteries of the universe? Great!

Let's start with a few clues and see what they uncover about these finances.

Here we go:

¢   Statement #1: "We've tried budgeting before, but it never works. It's pretty much a waste of time, since all of our money goes toward paying bills."

¢   Statement #2: "I don't get it. We make decent money but never feel like we can get ahead. Saving is not practical in our situation."

¢   Statement #3: "Bankers, the IRS, and mortgage lenders are all crooks! If we could just figure out how to get rid of them all, life would be great!"

So, given the above clues, could we hypothesize about the mystery of these households' personal finances that are not working out?

Each statement reveals some pretty dysfunctional personal finance thinking.

Statement #1 reveals that for this couple, a bill is a bill is a bill. There is no difference between one bill and another. They are all equally important in the eyes of these egalitarians. In their way of thinking, if they incur an expense that turns into a regular bill, that expense is now a need and no longer a consequence of succumbing to the want or impulse that led to the bill. In reality, if we were this couple, we'd know that monthly rent/mortgage is a need, monthly utility bills (electricity, gas, water, sewer, and trash) are essentially needs as well, communications are a high-priority want for most households, and television, Internet movie subscriptions, xyz-of-the-month services, and most other fixed monthly contracted services should be open for debate and negotiation as to how much we want them.

Statement #2 reveals what many of us feel. It's no surprise for most of us that the problem for this couple is not in their income. It's a spending and commitment problem. At virtually any income, we need to make a commitment to save if we want it to happen.

Saving money never happens on its own. It takes will.

Statement #3, while revealing a bit of borderline paranoia, is not as uncommon as hoped. One really bad experience with any of these entities can lead to a lifelong blame game where we play the role of helpless and stranded victim oppressed by the big, bad banker, government bureaucrat, or mortgage broker who is always on the prowl for our hard-earned money. The reality is that we are all personally responsible for our own financial success.

That said, what do all three statements have in common? They each indicate those who have not come to accept that not all expenses have been created equally and that it is spending behavior (much more so than earning ability) that has the greatest impact on financial success.

Without considering which expenses are or should be a priority, we can easily allow any bill delivered to our Inbox or Mailbox take precedence in financial decisions. Rather, by controlling spending and prioritizing expenses, we can banish those purchases from our finances that do not contribute to our identified measurements of financial success (a.k.a. written goals).

I suggest that we organize and prioritize expenses by using my quadrant system, included within the pages of this book.

QUOTE

Budgeting ensures that our money goes
to our priorities, not just our bills.

TODAY'S MONEY

Want or Need?

I live in the Boise, Idaho area. It's a wonderful place to live and raise a family. We have vibrant cities, four full seasons, incredible fishing, quick and easy access to beautiful mountains, rivers, dunes, and gorges. Unfortunately, we don't have it all. We are missing a vital component of most growing metropolitan areas around the country: a comprehensive public transportation system. It's not that our public transit officials haven't tried, but since our state constitution prohibits the collection of local taxes (county or city) that typically form the backbone of public transportation funding, we consequently have limited bus service and no rail, light rail, subway, or trolley services.

I share that prologue because we also have a geographically dispersed population. It's not uncommon to drive five or ten miles between recognizable population centers that share strong and interconnected economic ties. Consequently, there are many commuters that live fifty or even a hundred miles from their places of employment. Still, others live in remote towns and make weekly roundtrips of 200 to 300 miles just to shop at a discount warehouse or grocery stores.

So, it should not be surprising that, besides food and water, shelter and security, and some minimal amount of protective clothing, many of my students identify a car or truck as a survival need. I've had several adult students get a little hot under the collar when I've listed such transportation as a want rather than a need.

In my mind, though, needs are required for survival and do not involve any choice on our part as to whether we could get along without them. Could we live without water and food? Obviously not. What about shelter and the security it affords? Not for long. How about some clothing? Unless we're on a crazy Discovery Channel reality show, likely not (especially in colder climates). Then there are some medications and medical procedures that might be required. But what about a car? Could we survive without one? Do the circumstances requiring a car result from our own choices? Absolutely. Virtually the only justification given for classifying vehicles as a need is that "I need it to get to work." By extension, "If I can't get to work, I can't provide for the other needs in my household." This tends to negate that we have a choice in the matter. We choose to live in place A and work in place B. Regardless of how far apart A and B are, we had a choice in it. We could live closer to work or find a job closer to home, but that typically requires choosing to live in a smaller (sometimes significantly smaller) home. That's usually not something many are willing to do, not that we couldn't if physical survival were at stake.

The reason I insist on not classifying a car or a truck as a need is twofold: First, once we do, there is no longer any incentive to consider the alternatives. We don't look into public transportation options, into carpooling or ride sharing, or even pedal-powered transportation, each of which are generally more affordable than car ownership. Second, once we call a vehicle a need, it becomes far too easy to begin justifying spending more on it. "I need a car, so I might as well get a newer car, a faster car, a brighter, shinier, roomier, safer car. A more fuel efficient, louder, boom-boomier, chromier car." We end up spending significantly more on a mode of transportation than we otherwise would. So could we survive without a vehicle? Yes, but we (myself included) really, really, really, really wouldn't WANT to.

Step-by-Step Examining of the Expenses

¢ List all of the expenses you have each month as well as those you have had in the past three months.

¢ Categorize the expenses into needs or wants. Write "1" next to any need and write "2" next to a want. A need includes "physical survival" expenses as well as those required to sustain a minimal level of expected lifestyle.

¢ Categorize expenses (both needs and wants) as either an obligation (a recurring or contracted bill, usually with a set due date) or a discretionary expense (a purchase you are free to make anytime or not at all). Write "A" next to obligations and "B" next to discretionary expenses.

¢ Make a four-quadrant Payment Priority Chart by drawing a vertical line straight down the middle of a piece of paper and then drawing a horizontal line straight across the middle of the same paper (essentially, a cross). Label the top left quadrant as 1A, the top right quadrant as 1B, the bottom left quadrant as 2A and the bottom right quadrant as 2B.

¢ Looking at your list of expenses, write them into their corresponding quadrants. Within each quadrant (especially 2A and 2B), priority expenses from the most important to the least important.

Continue until all of your monthly expenses have been added to the chart.

You now have a visual plan of attack for paying your bills. Any expense in the 1A quadrant (top left) must absolutely get paid every month. Anything in the 1B quadrant (top right) should get paid also, but you can be flexible as to when it gets paid. Anything in the 2A quadrant (bottom left) should also be paid regularly, though you should aim to keep the number of expenses in this quadrant to a minimum. Finally, the 2B quadrant (bottom right) will contain expenses that can be removed from your budget whenever you have a financially rough month.

Dos and Don'ts

▲ Do reevaluate your needs and top priority wants, formally or informally, each year or so.

▲ Do make it a goal to cut out one expense from quadrant 2A and up to three expenses from quadrant 2B each month for the next six months.

▲ Do share the Needs versus Wants quadrants principle with your children, if applicable, starting around the age of eight years old or so.

▽ Don't get rid of all of your wants. You've got to live a little!

▽ Don't forget to include the financial needs and wants of your spouse or children.

▽ Don't justify spending on a want because "your situation is unique." If you try to justify a want as a need, it's a sign that a reality check is in order.

FACTOID

It is not surprising that many among us struggle to differentiate between our wants and needs. After all, according to Capital One's 2012 Back-to-School Shopping Survey, more than 30 percent of parents didn't even have a discussion with their children about needs versus wants before shopping for the school year.

22

THE FINANCIAL PATH OF LEAST RESISTANCE

There are many things in this world that flow towards the area of least resistance. Some of the more common ones are water, electricity, our thoughts, and our money. Water really doesn't have much to do with our discussion here. Our thoughts and our money, however, do.

While there is a time and place for all things under the sun, letting thoughts wander aimlessly accomplishes little when it comes to reaching financial goals. Dreamers dream; doers do.

We've already talked about setting goals and looking at them regularly. That should take care of our wandering thoughts. But what about our wandering money? What am I talking about when I say it flows in the direction of least resistance? Like the water in an irrigation ditch, money needs to have barriers placed in strategic locations to keep it flowing into our highest priorities, in this instance, our goals. Without these barriers, our money will seep (or more likely spill) out of a wallet like water into a dry desert plain.

Where are these holes in our budget? All we have to do is to look around us. They're practically everywhere. Any want or perceived want that we have (or that our children have, if we are parents) can become a leak in our budget. Every time we compare ourselves to neighbors or family or friends, particularly with regards to what we own and possess, we open up huge gaps in our financial ditch. "Did you hear what so-and-so just bought?" "Guess where the so-and-sos are heading on vacation?" All too often, such questions lead to feelings of either social and financial inferiority ("I'm not as valued by society as so-and-so if I don't own what they own.") or desires for unmerited rewards ("I work harder than he does, so why should he get to have all the fun?") or both.

In these cases, budget leaks can lead to huge one-time purchases of special vacations, a new vehicle, garage toys (a.k.a. all terrain vehicles, snowmobiles, boats, motorcycles, etc.), or other items and activities that may, in some cases, even promote family unity. They always lower our net worth and eat up any savings and credit card limits.

If we were to set up spending barriers in a strategic manner, these barriers will allow our financial future to grow, flourish, and prosper. What are these barriers that we should build and how do we do it? By writing down goals, we've already dug the ditch and have excavated the path where we'd like our money to flow.

We'll still need to work regularly to ensure that our money actually arrives at our goals.

Set up our barriers by completing the step-by-step budget barriers worksheet within this book.

TODAY'S MONEY

How Not To Budget

Around the era when dinosaurs ruled the earth, I went to college full-time in the afternoon and evenings and worked part-time in the mornings. I left home around 6:30 each weekday, rode my junker of a motorcycle six miles to my office in rain or shine (although I remember the snowy, cold, and dark mornings with particular pleasure), and then headed to campus just before lunch time. By the time I finished my projects, homework, and on-campus study, it might have been nine o'clock in the evening or later. Oh, what great times!

I share this because I got myself into a few bad habits that I justified because of my long days. Since I was not in the habit of retiring to my bed very early in college, I was usually pretty tired the next morning and didn't always have the energy to make myself breakfast before jumping on the motorcycle. Nor did I ever make myself a brown bag lunch to carry with me to campus. Apparently, I felt that brown bag lunches were for freshmen who weren't working and earning such a fortune as I was (ha!). As a consequence, I got in the habit of heading straight to the Holiday Oil station in front of my work each morning so I could buy an ultra-mega-giant-uber-grande soft drink and a six-pack of what I still lovingly refer to as chocolate wax donuts. Mmmmm!

Once on campus, I'd head for the campus cafeteria to buy a delicious Navajo taco or a less-than-healthy alternative. By the time I got out of class and was studying, I would stop at a vending machine or two (or five) for a candy bar, soft drink, or other snack to "tide me over." In today's dollars, I was likely spending $70 each week for what can only loosely be termed as two-and-a-half meals per day.

My justification was simple: I'm too busy and tired to eat breakfast at home, make and take a brown bag lunch and snacks to get me through until dinner. The reality was that I had stayed up longer than I needed to, I watched more football and *X-Files* than I should have, and I was so poorly organized when I went grocery shopping that I didn't purchase food appropriate for taking on campus. If I had been even more honest with myself, I would have admitted that I didn't want my friends and classmates to see me carrying a brown bag lunch around because I, from my own point of view, saw the brown bag lunch as something that was for children.

If I had recognized and accepted these pressures, I would have had greater motivation to shop better, eat healthier, and likely save about fifty dollars a week in today's money, or $1,500 per school year. Ouch! If I had only set up my own spending barriers, I could have invested that $1,500 per year rather than putting it on credit cards and paying interest for several years. My cost for eating wax donuts and Navajo tacos works out today to have been well over $100,000!!!

Step-by-Step Budgeting

Using the following steps, set up budget barriers that will maximize your chances to actually reach your financial goals.

1. Be honest with yourself.

2. In column 1, write down two or three Dollar Dumps (see preceding chapter) that you regularly spend money on. Also include some big ticket items that are tempting you to spend

lots of money in the coming year but that you really can't afford (e.g., snowmobiles, a big vacation, new car, etc.).

3. In column 2, write down how often you spend money on the item in column 1.

4. In column 3, write down how much you typically spend on each item in column 1. Decide how much of that money you prefer go to your established goals.

5. In column 4, write down the honest reasons to spend the money listed in column 3 (e.g., addiction, habit, social pressure, nostalgia for something from childhood, a way to pass the time, etc.).

6. Here's the toughest step. Looking down the road to when you will be tempted to spend money on the items in column 1, determine a way to overcome the temptation and write it down in column 5. This could include calling a family member or friend for support (to talk you out of it), moving the money to a hard-to-reach account (online or a certificate of deposit), or posting photos of your established financial goals around your home or office to remind you of what you really want to do.

7. Finally, share your goals with at least one family member or friend who will be your "budget fan" and cheer you on to reaching those goals.

Spending Barriers Worksheet

Dollar Dumps & Big Ticket Temptations	Frequency or Dates of Expenses	$ Amounts	Reasons for Spending	Counter-measures	Shared with Support

---

FINANCIAL FACTOID

According to the 2012 Consumer Financial Literacy Survey by the National Foundation for Credit Counseling and the Network Branded Prepaid Card Association, only 43 percent of US adults use a budget regularly. Additionally, 22 percent essentially admit that they have no idea how much money they spend on housing, food, and entertainment.

Dos and Don'ts

▲ Do keep your short-term goals at hand when working on spending barriers.

▲ Do choose a budget fan who will be both honest with you and supportive of your goals.

▲ Do revisit your Spending Barriers Worksheet monthly to begin with, but at least twice annually.

▽ Don't consider the Spending Barriers Worksheet as something to do in your head. Writing things down carries REAL power.

▽ Don't blame poor spending on lack of time or energy.

▽ Don't hide this worksheet from a spouse or children if applicable. Their support can be invaluable.

23

FOOLING YOUR FAMILY MEMBERS INTO BETTER FINANCIAL BEHAVIORS

Now that we've made it through most, if perhaps not all, of the chapters of this book with its various suggestions and have hopefully found additional motivation to make positive changes in our personal finances, we may be asking ourselves something like this:

"These ideas are all well and fine, and they'll probably even work, but the financial success of my household doesn't just depend upon my own habits and behaviors. I am married and have children who have a huge impact on our finances. When it comes to controlling spending and managing our money, what can I do to get them on board?"

The following ideas and suggestions are for all of the spouses and parents who wish they could get their husband, wife, or children to be more involved in and committed to reaching financial goals that benefit the household. None of the following come with a guarantee to convert the overspender or undisciplined spender into a budget-minded, goal-oriented team player. The key is finding the motivation for our loved ones' financial behaviors and using that towards the benefit of the entire household.

The Spontaneous Spending Spouse:

"My spouse values spontaneity. What can we do so that she lives within our household spending plan, but at the same time keeps spontaneity alive? When we've tried budgets before, they only made our relationship regimented and more stressful."

Contrary to popular belief, you can live within a spending plan while still maintaining a healthy degree of spontaneity. The key is to add to the budget what I call "fun money" or "guilt-free money."

Often, the problem is that one spouse will try to forecast every single monthly expense, including entertainment or recreation. This is a noble effort, except that the other spouse (the one who values being spontaneous) will seemingly do everything they can to NOT live by their spouse's plan. The situation drives both nuts. Fun money–guilt-free money-is the compromise solution. The Planner Spouse sets a certain amount of money aside for the next month that can be spent whenever and however the Spontaneous Spouse chooses (both spouses should theoretically get some fun money each month, whether it's five dollars or fifty dollars). This will satisfy the Planner Spouse's urge to be prepared for virtually every expense. The Spontaneous Spouse should find this arrangement satisfactory since there is now money to spend to his or her heart's content.

Here's where the guilt-free part comes in. At the end of the month, if one spouse approaches the other and asks what the fun money was spent on, here's the suggested response: Take your spouse by the hand, look your spouse right in the eye and say, "Sweetheart, I love you. I love you more than the day we met. I'm so glad we're together. And to answer your question about what I did with my fun money this month . . . it's none of your business."

Listen up, Planner Spouse. If you insist on receiving an accounting of where your spouse spent her fun money, you will turn that fun money into not-so-fun money. If it's spent on herself, wish her well. If it's spent on you or the kids, thank her for it. If she won't reveal her spending, leave it alone. That's the whole purpose of fun money.

Now listen up, Spontaneous Spouse. If you're in a committed relationship, it's time to include finances in that relationship. Spontaneity is great if it doesn't hurt anyone. Spending money on a whim when that money was intended for an important financial goal that your spouse identified hurts. Use the fun money to satisfy the urge for spontaneity, but don't confuse it with reckless abandon.

The Splurging Spouse:

"My spouse doesn't just value spontaneity. He thinks that he should be free to purchase a new vehicle, new motorcycle, new boat, new snowmobile, a new gaming system, or other expensive "toy" whenever the whim hits him. Since he works hard, he wants to play hard. I'm all for rewarding him for his hard work, but we can't afford all of the stuff he is continually buying. Please help!"

Splurging Spouses can be much more difficult to satisfy than the Spontaneous Spouse, since the size of their purchases can do dramatically greater damage to long-term finances than smaller spontaneous purchases. There is no easy or foolproof answer to this one, since the spending motivations usually come from deep within the Splurging Spouse. The impulse to spend large amounts of money is not an intellectual exercise. They typically know they can't afford the purchase, but rationalize it because of a perceived need in their minds. I'm not going to say that everyone who splurges or falls victim to a large impulse purchase needs this psychological help, but such repeated splurges tend to be indicators of some pretty severe self-centeredness and immaturity or, in extreme cases, symptoms of far deeper issues that the Splurging Spouse may need to address with the help of a professional counselor.

There are entire books and a number of other experts who deal solely with this issue, including Furnham and Argyle's *The Psychology of Money*, Mellan's *Money Harmony*, Pulliam Weston's *Changing Your Mind's Spending Attitudes*, and *The Journal of Consumer Psychology*.

One telling sign of being married to a Splurging Spouse is if you feel that you constantly have to say "no" to your spouse's requests to spend money. Splurging Spouses can sometimes sound like a child coming to a parent for money to buy a piece of candy. Or, they might feel that asking for forgiveness after making the purchase will be easier than asking for permission. Or, they may, in extreme cases, try to hide their purchases. In spite of the preceding disclaimer, there is a way to help Splurging Spouses curb their destructive behavior, and that is through holding them accountable for their own actions.

Start with both spouses sitting down and setting and agreeing to mutually-beneficial financial goals.

Next, post those goals where both of you will see them regularly.

Then, agree to meet at the same time on the same day EVERY week for a fifteen-minute financial huddle. During those fifteen minutes, review your mutually-agreed upon goals, ensure that your checking account is balanced, and determine how all of your bills in the next week or so will be paid.

Then return to your goals and talk about what will be done that week to make those goals a reality.

Often, involving Splurging Spouses in financial management activities, even as small and relatively pain-free as the financial huddle, will help them feel more connected to their own actions. By establishing goals, both spouses have set either implied or specific spending limitations. The biggest challenge comes with setting consequences to any choice that wanders from these goals.

Splurging Spouses needs to know that when they spend money on something that is not in the household budget, there will be negative consequences down the road. Will it mean you won't be able to take a family vacation this year? You won't be able to fix up the yard? Whatever the consequence, write down a list of activities or purchases that will be in jeopardy if both spouses do not stick to the spending plan. Just make sure that such consequences are meaningful (i.e., painful) to both spouses. Ideally, keep that list with your goals sheet.

The Resistant Spouse:

> *"What can I do to get my spouse on board with these ideas?*
> *She resists all attempts to control her spending."*

Use this simple trick to motivate a Resistant Spouse to become your partner in budgeting, saving, and paying off debts, rather than remaining an adversary through unplanned spending.

Let the Resistant Spouse know that each time the household pays off a debt, she will receive a one-time bonus the following month equivalent at most to the monthly payment that was being sent to the debt that was just paid off. If, for example, you paid off a debt whose monthly payment was $150, the Resistant Spouse, as a reward for otherwise living within the spending plan, will be given $150 the next month to spend however she wants, no questions asked. The challenge is to not make her feel guilty for how she spends that $150. Otherwise, she'll feel duped and won't continue to participate in the future.

If the household somehow doesn't have debt (not common with Resistant Spouses in the home), set periodic savings goals and treat them much the same as paying off a debt. Once a goal is reached, the monthly contribution (or a portion thereof) goes to the Resistant Spouse to use according to his or her desires.

Some reading this may think this is bribery. I used to think the same, until my friend, Jim, shared a priceless thought with me. We were discussing some parenting challenges and how I hated to "reward" our son each time he did something he was supposed to be doing anyway. To me, that reward felt equivalent to a bribe. Jim, in his experience and wisdom, said something along the lines of, "A bribe is money given to another in order to get them to do something illegal. Rewarding good behavior is not a bribe, but behavioral motivation." So, don't look at it as a bribe. Remember that the purpose is to get both spouses on the same financial page, and working toward the same financial goals. If the Resistant Spouse requires a reward, so be it ... so long as he or she is contributing to your financial success.

Children:

"How can I help my child(ren) develop better financial attitudes and habits?"

We can help our children develop a healthy relationship with money using some pretty simple (and fun) tactics. First, I would consider myself a poor financial educator if, after all I have written about helping to prepare for and assure a better financial future, I didn't look at our true future: the next generation. Even if we don't have children of our own, we likely have grandchildren, nieces, and nephews or there are children of our friends whom we consider to be family. Whether in our home or in our village, we all have children that look to us, for better or for worse, as adult role models. These children need our help and guidance, especially when it comes to money management. While every child is different, we'll find some general guidelines for talking to the children at various stages of their lives.

Early in children's lives, up to the age of eight or so, they are in observation mode. It is critical that what we do and say during these years builds an understanding of important, healthy personal finance behaviors, as well as a belief and confidence in their ability to succeed financially as they grow.

As they enter the "tween" years (ages eight to twelve), they need to be given opportunities to provide input and make very basic financial decisions that affect them directly. If we're going to give a child an allowance, it is during this age that I suggest we start doing so. Why not earlier? Because before the age of eight, children have no real concept of the value of money. If they can't count to a thousand or know what a million is, they're probably not ready to handle varying quantities of money. However, if earlier in their lives, we give them dimes and nickels and quarters to spend on various candies or toy dispensers, they will be more likely to understand what coin gets them the bigger or better toy. However, during the tween years, besides an allowance, parents, grandparents, and other adults need to allow the children to begin making some of their own small financial mistakes. This is one of the most difficult lessons that we, the adults, need to learn as well.

Virtually all of us learn a great deal from our mistakes. If we don't allow children to make mistakes with a small amount of money (say, wasting it on a piece of candy rather than saving it to get the toy or game they really want), then they will be ripe for making huge financial mistakes when they head off to college or move out on their own (say, maxing out a credit card or draining their checking account for an immediate want rather than for their established financial priorities).

For our teens and young adults, our challenges as parents and influential adults become even more critical. We have a tendency to want to fix all of their problems or make sure they avoid them. We want them to focus on their schoolwork, so we often discourage them from getting part-time jobs that would detract from their homework, sports, and other school-related activities. While there are studies1 that indicate college students working more than twenty hours per week are less likely to graduate, I believe that having a part-time job, which does not interfere with coursework and study time, will actually increase enrollment retention. Anytime we invest our own time and efforts into an activity, we're much more likely to see it through.

To summarize, there is no better teacher than experience. From a young age, children need to be working toward financial success (and experiencing small financial failures) so they will be better prepared to live independently and self-sufficiently. Our role, as influential adults in their lives, is to model healthy financial habits and attitudes, teach them directly and indirectly about being a consistent saver and a wise consumer, and show them what we mean by budgeting, managing our money, planning for the future, setting limits to our spending, and preparing for future purchases.

We will never regret the time spent financially mentoring the next generation, whereas we will all regret neglecting these opportunities.

TODAY'S MONEY

Fooling Family Members

I facilitated a budgeting class recently at a large corporation's "school" for their local employees, and I spoke with a young lady afterwards (we'll call her Jaiden) who expressed a frustration I hear far too often from spouses. This is an equal opportunity frustration in that it does not affect one gender disproportionately. It does tend to cause more problems among younger couples than older ones, but that may be due to the likelihood that young couples in such circumstances will not stay together long enough to become an older couple if they don't deal with the issue.

To all but quote Jaiden, "Do you have any suggestions for my husband and me? I'm really good with my money. I do not buy frivolous things. I hate debt. I shop with a list. I do all the things budget counselors would tell me to do. My husband, on the other hand, has no such desire, no such training, no such restraint; he believes money is to be spent on living now and not saved for what may or may not happen later."

I could hear the helplessness in Jaiden's voice, calling for any magic pill I could prescribe for her husband. Unfortunately, there's no single answer for everyone. I do have several suggestions and ideas to pursue in such situations, and I'm hoping one or more of them helped Jaiden's husband bridle his overspending passions.

Step-by-Step

To help get both spouses on the same financial page of their proverbial relationship book, here are a few activities to choose from:

1. **The Five-Step Values Approach**

    I. Individually, write down a list of ten of your most important life values. What do we want out of life? How do we want the epitaph on our grave to read? "Here lies me. In life, I knew how to…?" For example, his might include "Have a Family, Grow, Love, Have Fun, Be Independent, Have Pleasure, and Rest." Hers might include "Be Safe, Love, Create, Build Unity, Trust, Have Faith, Have a Family, and Prosper." For sample lists, just Google "List of Personal Values." I like the list put together by Charlotte Roberts in *The Fifth Discipline Fieldbook*, but your lists don't have to come from a textbook.

    II. Circle the top three most important values.

    III. Sit down together with your original list of ten important values and top three values and share them with your spouse. You may be surprised, or the experience may simply confirm your view of your spouse.

    IV. While it may be easy to contrast our opposing values (e.g. Independence-Togetherness or Stability-Excitement or Adventure-Rest), the goal of this exercise is to compare our similar values (e.g. Love-Family-Home-Affection or Excitement-Fun-Pleasure) or at least somewhat related values (e.g. Status-Respect-Friendship-Admiration).

    V. Finally, here comes the kicker. Discuss how money affects each of these shared and contrasting values. Does spending money contribute to realizing these values in your lives? Does it detract from their realization?

2. The Incentivization (Not Bribery)
Approach to Paying off Debt or Building Savings

I. Especially effective for spouses who love to spend but who also express remorse for overspending!

II. Set up either a debt elimination strategy or a savings strategy. These should include monthly payments or deposits toward the debt elimination or savings goals.

III. Ideally, your strategy should involve a debt being liquidated (zeroed out) or a savings goal being reached every three to four months or less.

IV. Approach your spouse with a "Win-Win" deal. If your spouse will help you both stay within your strategy by controlling household spending, then each time you pay off a debt, he or she will be rewarded the next month with that debt's monthly payment to spend however he or she so chooses, without any guilt-trip from you. The case would be the same for savings. Each time you reach a savings goal, your spouse gets that savings contribution the following month, no questions asked. Each of these incentives are only good for one month, but by the time you've paid off ALL of your debt or reached SEVERAL of your savings goals, it's more likely than not that your spouse will have curbed their overspending and realized the value and satisfaction of living within a plan.

3. The Awareness Approach
This approach addresses the spouse who loves to "live for the moment."

I. Determine how much money you're spending as a household on interest and fees each month and over a year's time.

II. Return to the Introduction's Value of Money discussion to determine how many hours you and/or your spouse must be at work in order to earn enough just to cover the cost of interest and fees you pay each month.

III. Sit down with your spouse and voice to them your recognition of the importance of living in the moment. You will have no success if you approach them with the attitude that they need to change or that they're wrong for acting in such a way. The success of this approach comes from the spouse becoming aware of the financial impact of their actions, not from you pointing out such an impact.

IV. If your spouse loves going to the movies but typically puts such activities on a credit card that involves paying interest, consider the following approach: "Sweetheart, I think I've found a way for us to afford for you to go to an extra movie every month, without us having to earn any extra income." "No way," he or she will reply. Here's where you simply share (not "tell") that the amount of interest you're paying monthly on your credit card equals an extra movie ticket each month. Actually, it might equal much more than that, but this is just an example.

V. Once your spouse can relate the amount of interest you pay to something of immediate, personal, or real value to him or herself, they'll be more likely to see interest as something to be avoided rather than "just a part of life."

VI. If they need a little extra inducement, you could ask your spouse what they would rather be doing during all of the "extra" hours he or she has to work in order to pay for just your credit card interest, especially if they are the ones purporting to want to "live in the moment." "Wouldn't you rather be fishing? Or mountain biking? Or traveling?"

To help your children develop money smarts, here are a few activities to choose from:

1. **The Household Money Pot Activity**
   (children 8 years of age or older)

   I. We need to involve our children in the household budgeting decisions. We have to get over our fear of sharing how much money we earn (or don't earn). Explain to them that you trust that they will keep your family finances (income and expenses) within your household and not speak about them to others without your permission.

   II. Use Monopoly or other play money to go through your household's monthly budget.

   III. Count out your monthly gross income and place it in "the pot" at the center of the table.

   IV. Have your children remove your monthly expenses from the pot, one expense at a time.

   V. Explain the value and benefit to the family of each expense, including taxes, housing, groceries, savings, allowance, insurance, clothing, entertainment, gift giving, etc.

2. **Learning to Say "No" without Saying "No" (no age limitation)**

   I. As you take your children shopping, you need to avoid simply telling them "no" when they ask for something that costs money, even though you're effectively saying, "No."

   II. Worse yet, you need to avoid saying, "We can't afford that." Such responses can create in your children an attitude that money is a scarcity and that it should be spent immediately before it disappears.

III. Instead, try to respond with phrases such as, "That's not a financial priority right now." The end result is the same (you've answered, "No"), but you're helping the child begin to think about financial priorities.

3. **The TV or Radio Commercial Critic Game**
    (from ages 3 years and up)

    I. When a TV or radio commercial comes on, discuss with your children what the advertisers are trying to do.

    II. Are they suggesting that purchasing a particular toy, drinking a specific beverage, or participating in a certain activity will do away with all concerns and make us happy? Perhaps they are insinuating that wearing a certain brand of clothing will make us more popular and accepted?

    III. We need to help our children understand that advertisements (television, web, radio, billboard, etc.) are simply trying to get us to buy something that we really don't need. Such an activity can help us raise a healthy but skeptical (not cynical) consumer.

FACTOID

Of all the factors used to predict a marriage's dissolution (divorce), a longitudinal study by Paul Amato and Stacey Rogers found that only sexual infidelity or drug abuse by a spouse were stronger predictors of future divorce than believing that one's spouse spends money foolishly. Interestingly, this is particularly true if the pound-foolish spouse is the husband.

Dos and Don'ts

▲ Do get your spouse involved in the finances, even if it's just for a weekly "update."

▲ Do agree to common goals with your spouse, and post them where you'll both see them regularly.

▲ Do allow your children to make mistakes with their money when they're young.

▽ Don't require an accounting from your spouse of what they do with any "Fun Money" they get.

▽ Don't discourage entrepreneurship in your children.

▽ Don't focus on the negative financial behaviors of your spouse or children. Behaviors are typically outward expressions of internal values and beliefs.

CONCLUSION

Before we finish our everyday money experience together, I'd like to thank you for the time you've spent with me. Several chapters address topics that are pretty new to some, while others provide ideas and tips that the more experienced are going to be anxious to try out.

I also want to congratulate you for sticking with me. It's one thing to want to increase financial literacy and improve financial skills. It's a much bigger step to actually pick up a book and start doing something about it.

Having made it to the end of *Everyday Money for Everyday People*, you would do well to go back through the chapters and pick one topic to focus on each day or each week. Find the Step-by-Step and the Dos and Don'ts lists and commit to putting one or more of them into practice now, today! Like attending a workshop, if you don't put into practice your new knowledge within twenty-four hours, the more unlikely it will become that you ever will.

Finally, it's my hope that this book is just another step on your journey together toward financial stability and success. I encourage you to seek out and share further opportunities along the way. I'm not just referring to my *Everyday Money* books and programs or the classes I facilitate. Whether reading a personal finance book by another author, attending a workshop by other trusted financial experts, participating in a money management webinar, calling a credit counselor or financial advisor, or just talking to a family member or friend about the topic, let's all keep moving our everyday money skills forward.

END NOTES

Introduction

1. "Financial Capability Study." *FINRA Investor Education Foundation*. www.usfinancialcapability.org.

2. Eric Schlosser, *Fast Food Nation* (Houghton Mifflin, 2001), 42.

3. "Table 1: Annual Estimates of the Population for the United States, Regions, States, and Puerto Rico: April 1, 2010 to July 1, 2011." *US Census Bureau*. www.census.gov/popest/data/state/totals/2011/tables/NST-EST2011-01.xls.

4. "Payday Lending Demographic and Statistical Information: July 2000 through December 2009." *Colorodo UCCC*. www.coloradoattorneygeneral.gov/sites/default/files/uploads/DDLASummary2009corr.pdf.

5. "Mom and Dad 'MIA' on Teaching Money Management? Survey." *Visa*. www.practicalmoneyskills.com/about/press/releases_2011/0524.php.

6. "As High School Graduates Open their Gifts, Parents Have Key Opportunity to Talk Money Management." Capital One. http://phx.corporate-ir.net/phoenix.zhtml?c=70667&p=irol-newsArticle&ID=1573673&highlight.

Chapter 2

1. Stanley, Thomas, and William Danko. *The Millionaire Next Door* (Taylor Trade Publishing. 1996)

2. Scott Hankins, Mark Hoekstra and Paige Marta Skiba. "The Ticket to Easy Street The Financial Consequences of Winning the Lottery." *Vanderbilt Law and Economics Research Paper No. 10-12.* http://papers.ssrn.com/sol3/papers. cfm?abstract_id=1324845.

3. Pablo S. Tore. "How (and Why) Athletes Go Broke." *Sports Illustrated.* http://sportsillustrated.cnn.com/vault/article/ magazine/MAG1153364.

4. Vince Veneziani. "10 Lottery Winners Who Lost It All." *Business Insider.* www.businessinsider. com/10-lottery-winners-who-lost-it-all-2010-5?op=1.

5. "7 lotto winners who lost it all [Updated]." *The Week.* http://theweek.com/article/ index/203753/7-lotto-winners-who-lost-it-all-updated.

6. Pablo S. Tore. "How (and Why) Athletes Go Broke." *Sports Illustrated.* http://sportsillustrated.cnn.com/vault/article/ magazine/MAG1153364.

Chapter 5

1. "Giving Statistics." *Charity Navigator.* www.charitynavigator.org/index.cfm?bay=content. view&cpid=42.

Chapter 6

1. Pablo S. Tore. "How (and Why) Athletes Go Broke." *Sports Illustrated.* http://sportsillustrated.cnn.com/vault/article/ magazine/MAG1153364.

Chapter 7

1. "Cost of Living." *Cost of Living.* http://thecostofliving.com/index.
   php?id=147. "GE Monitor Top Refrigerator." *Industrial Designers
   Society of America.*
   http://www.idsa.org/ge-monitor-top-refrigerator-1927.

Chapter 8

1. Drazen Prelec and Duncan Simester, "Always Leave Home
   Without It: A Further Investigation of the Credit-Card Effect on
   Willingness to Pay." *Marketing Letters,* 2001, Vol. 12, No. 1, 5-12.

2. Joydeep Srivastava and Priya Raghubir, "Debiasing Using
   Decomposition: The Case of Memory-Based Credit Card
   Expense Estimates." *Journal of Consumer,* 2002 Vol. 12 No. 3,
   262. http://groups.haas.berkeley.edu/marketing/PAPERS/
   PRIYA/p3.pdf.

3. Tamara Holmes. "Credit Cards Can Make You Fat."
   Bank Rate. www.bankrate.com/nltrack/news/
   cc/20070704_credit_cards_fat_a1.asp.

4. "Lost or Stolen Credit, ATM, and Debit Cards."
   Federal Trade Commission. www.consumer.ftc.gov/
   articles/0213-lost-or-stolen-credit-atm-and-debit-cards.

5. "Behavior: The Role of Rehearsal and Immediacy of Payments."
   Journal of Consumer Research, Vol. 27, No. 4, March 2001.

Chapter 9

1. Factoid Priya Raghubir and Joydeep Srivastava. "The
   Denomination Effect." *Journal of Consumer Research.*
   www.jstor.org/stable/10.1086/599222.

Chapter 10

1. "2012 Christmas Gift Spending Plans Return to Pre-Recession Levels." *American Research Group*. http://americanresearchgroup.com/holiday.

Chapter 12

1. Al Bingham, Road to 850: *Proven Strategies for Increasing Your Credit Score* (Layton, UT: C.P. Publishing, 2007), 111-2.

Chapter 13

1. "History." *FICO*. www.fico.com/en/Company/Pages/history.aspx.

2. Lynn Langton. "Identity Theft Reported by Households, 2005-2010." *US Department of Justice*. http://www.bjs.gov/content/pub/pdf/itrh0510.pdf.

Chapter 16

1. "What's not in my FICO Score." *My FICO*. www.myfico.com/CreditEducation/WhatsNotInYourScore.aspx.

2. "Improve Your Score." *My FICO*. www.myfico.com/crediteducation/improveyourscore.aspx.

Chapter 17

1. Elizabeth Mendes. "Americans Spend $151 a Week on Food; the High-Income, $180." *Gallup*. www.gallup.com/poll/156416/americans-spend-151-week-food-high-income-180.aspx.

Chapter 23

1. Russell Rumberger and Sun Ah Lim. "Why Students Drop Out of School: A Review of 25 Years of Research." *California Dropout Research Project*. http://www.spokanecounty.org/data/juvenile/modelsforchange/School%20dropouts%20-%20Why%20sudents%20dropout%20of%20school.pdf.

ACKNOWLEDGMENTS

I wish to personally thank the following individuals. Without their inspiration, contributions, and support, this book would not have been written:

Joseph Cestaro, Thomas Drechsler, and the rest of the fantastic team at Debt Reduction Services Inc., (there are too many to list here) for allowing me to do what I love;

Maryanna Young who inspired me to write and to do it now;

Amy Larson for bringing clarity and succinctness to my ramblings;

My fellow Aloha group members, Aspen, Tobe, Cindy, and Shannon for helping me stay grounded and for encouraging me to keep moving forward;

My parents, who have always inspired me toward greater knowledge, better habits, and real wisdom;

Most of all, to My Loves, Wendy, and our four beautiful children who make life worth living and who motivate all of my work.

ABOUT THE AUTHOR

Author and Certified Personal Finance Counselor®, Todd R. Christensen, MA, CPFFE, is Director of Education for the National Financial Education Center at Debt Reduction Services. Inc., a nationwide, nonprofit credit counseling agency. Author of *Everyday Money for Everyday People* (2013), Todd develops educational programs and produces materials that teach personal financial skills and responsibilities. He facilitates hundreds of workshops annually to thousands of individuals regarding the fundamentals of effective money management.

He currently serves as president-elect of the Idaho Jump$tart Coalition, chair of the Ethics Committee for the Association for Financial Counseling and Planning Education, a member of the Council for Certification of the American Association of Family and Consumer Sciences, and as a member of the program coordinating committees of three southwest Idaho housing authorities.

Todd relishes speaking to large groups, such as the Smart Women Smart Money conference in Boise, Idaho, in 2012 and a general session of the Association for Financial Counseling and Planning Education in Jacksonville, Florida, in 2011. His published articles and booklets have addressed topics ranging from marriage and money to raising financially smart children, and recovering from bankruptcy to controlling holiday spending.

Todd also served in 2009 as a volunteer Spanish and French language interpreter at the Special Olympics 2009 World Winter Games in Boise, in 2008 as an evaluator of the Pre-Professional Certification Test for the American Association of Family and Consumer Sciences, and has served frequently as a financial education awards judge for various conferences and associations. In 2007, he helped to draft the course standards for Idaho's Mathematics of Personal Finance high school class. An Eagle Scout himself, he has also served in adult leadership positions in scouting.

He thrives on speaking at large conferences and small meetings and facilitating classroom presentations at all levels.